ACCLAIM FOR *INTANGIENCE*

In *Intangience*, Ernie Ross integrates rigorous academic work with decades of experience across business, politics, and culture. Ross offers a compelling exploration of the invisible language that connects us—what I would call the "intangible architecture" of human flourishing. With intellectual rigor and the heart of a storyteller, Ross provides a framework for understanding how we create value not just in markets, but in minds and hearts. This book is an essential read for anyone committed to building deeper connections—in business, in leadership, and in life.

—Dr. Tal Ben Shahar
Cofounder, Happiness Studies Academy; Former Harvard University Lecturer, Positive Psychology; Best-selling author of Happiness, Being Happy *and several other books*

I've had the privilege of working with Ernie Ross in Paris and witnessing firsthand his Intangience framework in action—both in a training and a masterclass. In a world flooded with noise, this book unveils the hidden language of human connection that gives real meaning—and value—to brands, relationships, and ideas. More than ever, companies need to leverage thoughtful messaging that connects deeply and meaningfully with audiences. Ernie's work is a vital guide for anyone who wants to communicate with purpose and craft messages that truly resonate.

—Prof. Alon Rozen

Dean, CEO, president, and professor of innovation, École des Ponts Business School, Paris, France

Ernie Ross and the team from Intangience have developed a very powerful framework for adding purpose, values, connection and heart to the dialogue forward-thinking brands are having with their communities.

—Dr. Guila Kessous

Harvard Business Review, French human rights activist, UNESCO Artist for Peace

I was truly impressed by the Intangience MasterClass, with the insights shared that are redefining the world as we know it. As a client, we have applied the principles of the award-winning methodology to our brands and can attest to the impact, success, and profitability it has brought to our company over the years.

—Clifford Reis

Chairman and managing director, Banks DIH Limited, Guyana

We have entrusted our key brands and global campaigns to the novel Intangience process. It seems to have a knack for accurately framing complex communication challenges so that the right solutions and strategies emerge.

—Anthony Sabga III

CEO, Ansa McAL Group

I was so impressed by the results of the Intangience branding methodology, I took the decision to immerse all senior members of staff in it across all territories in which we operate.

—Ravi Tewari

Group CEO, executive director, Guardian Group

A projected 2.5 percent decline on Mainstream Beer (CARIB, CARIB Light, and Stag) due to the pandemic was converted into a 10.3 percent increase over the sales of the previous year. We don't always know the strength and power that GREAT marketing and communications have on us until we see communication like this!

—Robin Cumberbatch

Sales director, CARIB Brewery Limited

This powerful insight is critical to anyone who needs to promote their organization, services, or products. My personal experience is that understanding the principles of Intangience has made a world of difference in my ability to communicate the story of the UPEACE Centre for Executive Education.

—Mohit Mukherjee
Founder of Centre for Executive Education, United Nations established University for Peace

INTANGIENCE

ERNIE ROSS

NTANGIENCE

NTANGIENCE

HOW HUMAN CONNECTION CREATES VALUE BETWEEN PEOPLE, BRANDS, AND IDEOLOGIES

NTANGIENCE
NTANGIENCE
NTANGIENCE
NTANGIENCE

Forbes | Books

Published by Forbes Books, Charleston, South Carolina.
An imprint of Advantage Media Group.

Printed in the United States of America.

10 9 8 7 6 5 4 3 2 1

ISBN: 979-8-88750-631-9 (Hardcover)
ISBN: 979-8-88750-632-6 (eBook)

Library of Congress Control Number: 2025908624

Cover design by Matthew Morse.
Layout design by Ruthie Wood.
Illustrations by Wesley Strickland.

07-21-2025 10:41

To Bryan Davis, who introduced me to the whole idea of intangible values and guided me on its significance in my work. His genius lives on through the methodology I developed in response to his initial nudge to the subject matter.

To my daughter, Lael-Anne, who inspired me to write this book as my legacy to her own studies in the field of human connection. I'm sure her highly intelligent mind will identify other unique patterns and bring new insights far beyond my own.

To my mum, who would have been so proud to see this publication and say, "I must have done something right." Your sacrifices live on, Mum.

To my second dad, Tony Cole, who raised my siblings and me as his own. You imbued each of us with the true meaning of unconditional love. We thrive because of you.

And to my dad, whose intellect and writing ability impressed and inspired me from an early age. This book is dedicated to his pride and belief in me.

In memory of my brother Alan.

INTANGIENCE

INTANGIENCE
INTANGIENCE
INTANGIENCE
INTANGIENCE
INTANGIENCE
INTANGIENCE
INTANGIENCE
INTANGIENCE
INTANGIENCE
INTANGIENCE
INTANGIENCE

CONTENTS

FOREWORD XIII
by Mohit Mukherjee

INTRODUCTION 1

CHAPTER ONE 11
How to Survive in a Country Where Eating Bread Is Illegal

CHAPTER TWO 25
How to Sell Used Toothbrushes

CHAPTER THREE 37
How to Create an Inspiring Movement

CHAPTER FOUR 55
How a Border Dispute Became a Beer War

CHAPTER FIVE 71
How Freedom of the Press Was Transformed
Into Freedom *From* the Press

CHAPTER SIX 83
How Gang Leaders in the Caribbean
Responded Positively to a Message

CHAPTER SEVEN 95
How to Develop a Sixth Sense of InvisAbility

CHAPTER EIGHT 111
How to Sell a Banana and Duct Tape for $6.2 Million

CHAPTER NINE 121
How to Redefine and Reframe Everything
to Discover the Right Answer

CHAPTER TEN 129
How It All Started

EPILOGUE 141

INDEX 145

FOREWORD

BY MOHIT MUKHERJEE

Personal Connection

I consider Ernie Ross a visionary in the truest sense—someone who doesn't just see things as they are, but sees what they *could* be. When Ernie and I first connected, I was leading the United Nations University for Peace's Centre for Executive Education, an initiative I had founded and believed in deeply. But as is often the case with founders, I was too close to see its full potential. Ernie saw it instantly.

Drawing on the very *Intangience* principles he outlines in this book, Ernie guided my team in identifying the intangible values at the heart of our work and showed us how to express them in ways that truly resonate with our audience. It was that transformative half-day session that reshaped our messaging going forward from traditional communication to *compelling* connection. Our impact, reach, and ability to connect with people around the world have all been elevated because of his insight and generosity.

A short story of Ernie's vision and drive: During the early days of the pandemic in 2020, he spearheaded a powerful collaboration between the UPEACE Centre and the Guardian Group that resulted in one of the most aspirational and impactful projects I've been part of in my entire career, titled "Pandemic of Performance." It was a regional initiative that guided small businesses and entrepreneurs on how to turn adversity into an advantage. That initiative didn't just inform or inspire; it uplifted and united. It was a masterclass in *Intangience* in action!

Why This Book Matters

It's from this place of deep respect and admiration that I'm honored to introduce *Intangience.*

In a world overflowing with messages, brands, and ideas all competing for our attention, it's easy to believe that louder is better and that success is measured purely in metrics. But as *Intangience* so powerfully illustrates, the things that truly move us are often unseen, unmeasured, and—until now—largely unspoken.

What Ernie unpacks for us in this book is a powerful methodology—a blend of neuroscience, storytelling, and Ernie's decades of on-the-ground experience—that can transform the way we think about communication. At its core, *Intangience* is about unlocking the shared values that connect us to one another—values like belonging, hope, and purpose.

Ernie's career spans continents and sectors. He has helped elect heads of state, guided social change initiatives (I was fortunate to witness this first hand at UPEACE), and turned ordinary products into beloved brands. Ernie's approach is one of deep listening and empathy. Whether he's speaking to a consumer, a voter, a team, or a community, his first instinct is to ask: What matters most to them? What story are they already living? And how can we connect to it, authentically and with care? This is the approach of *Intangience* and the "science of human connection." And it's a skill set more urgently needed than ever!

Call To Action

We are living in an age when trust is fractured, attention is fleeting, and many of our institutions are struggling to stay relevant. Leaders, brands, and change-makers who want to thrive in this environment must go beyond slogans and strategies. They must speak the language of connection. That language is *Intangience*, anchored in the three schools of Pillars of Purpose, Currency of Conversation, and the Science of Human Connection.

So, whether you're a brand strategist, an entrepreneur, a nonprofit leader, a political campaigner, or simply someone who wants to lead more intentionally, this book offers more than tools—it offers a new paradigm. The timing could not be better for Ernie to extend his powerful approach by capturing it in this manual!

I am grateful—for Ernie's belief in me, for our collaboration, for the transformation he helped catalyze in our team, and for the friendship and example he continues to offer.

INTANGIENCE

INTANGIENCE
INTANGIENCE
INTANGIENCE
INTANGIENCE
INTANGIENCE
INTANGIENCE
INTANGIENCE
INTANGIENCE
INTANGIENCE
INTANGIENCE

INTRODUCTION

Not the ones speaking the same language, but the ones sharing the same feeling, understand each other.

—RUMI

"Let me tell you a story." These six simple words are an invitation, a hand extended, a request for engagement and connection.

On the remote island of Sulawesi in Indonesia, a cramped, damp cave contains a sketch of an ancient animal outlined in faded red—a curly-tailed creature connecting us to the people who lived in that place more than thirty-five thousand years ago.

A tanned leather sheet holds twenty-six recipes that share the secrets of summoning angelic powers through a thirteen-thousand-year-old blend of herbs and ritual prayers, connecting us to the eighth-century Egyptians who inscribed these invocations to inform and inspire.

Carefully woven and knotted strands of llama hair connect us to the Andean peoples who, some six thousand years ago, recorded data through each precise knot, communicating stories by a cord's length, spacing, and color.

There's a desire for connection that transcends the barriers of language, geography, and time—a desire to relate to other humans, other people, at a deeper level.

The Language of Connection

We speak this language of connection by focusing on what we hold in common rather than on what separates or divides us. This language of connection contains a vocabulary of shared values, communicating core messages about relationships, happiness, gratitude, and purpose. The decisions we make every day are driven by a desire for connection—to share our experiences of the world around us with others in a way that positively impacts them and links us more closely to a meaningful community.

These values are intangible. Things such as love, joy, security, and humor lack a physical presence, but their impact is very real. We want to be linked to others in a way that equips us to experience love or safety or community. These intangible values are also the building blocks of purpose, empowering individuals and organizations to become better by focusing on values that unify. These are the values that drive decision-making at every level, whether consciously or unconsciously.

There's a desire for connection that transcends the barriers of language, geography, and time—a desire to relate to other humans, other people, at a deeper level.

What makes a bottle of Coke, a beverage containing thirty-eight grams of sugar that *isn't marketed for flavor*, sell more than 1.9 billion units globally every single day? Coke is the embodiment of human connection and the joy that comes with it.

Nike isn't just quality athletic wear. It's the embodiment of self-actualization and personal achievement. It's even social activism. Without that iconic Swoosh logo, a Nike sneaker is just foam, fabric, and rubber. Add the logo, and its intangible value emerges to imbue the product with a whole new assessment of worth. So, it is the derivative meaning of intangible values that determines the worth of things more than anything else. This insight alters our understanding of what shapes the way we make choices about virtually everything that is traded.

In the world of politics, it is no different. The ability to weave compelling stories based upon shared intangible values determines the resonance of the message and the appeal of the candidate. Religious leaders are followed by believers in the intangible values espoused by the faith.

The stock market is a good example of how important intangible assets and values have become. The total value of the S&P 500 in November 2024 was about $45 trillion,[1] yet if you sold every physical asset traded, every product, factory, and office building, you wouldn't even get to 20 percent of the value.[2] So, if it can't be touched, weighed, held, or shipped, what is it? It's an intangible asset, often sold to consumers through shared intangible values.

---

1 "S&P 500 Market Cap (I:SP500MC)," YCHARTS, https://www.ycharts.com/indicators/sp_500_market_cap#:~:text=S%26P%20500%20Market%20Cap%20is,37.16T%20one%20year%20ago.

2 Sarah Ponczek, "Epic S&P 500 Rally Is Powered by Assets You Can't See or Touch," Bloomberg, October 21, 2020, https://www.bloomberg.com/news/articles/2020-10-21/epic-s-p-500-rally-is-powered-by-assets-you-can-t-see-or-touch.

TANGIBLE vs. INTANGIBLE ASSETS

Intangible assets currently account for **90%** of the S&P 500's total assets.

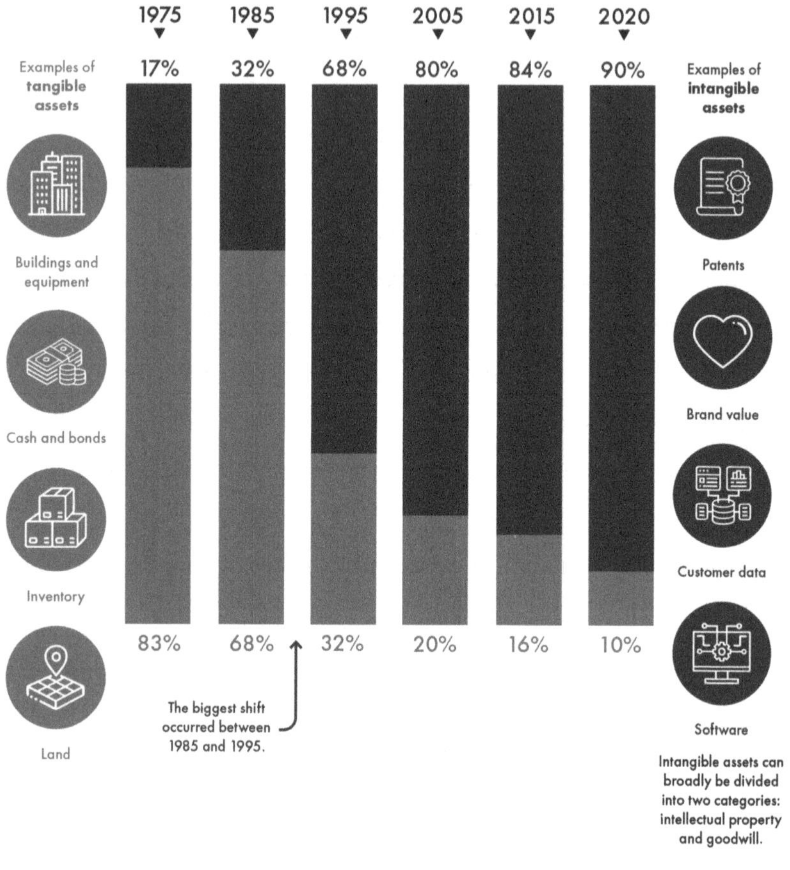

Source: "Intangible Asset Market Value Study," Ocean Tomo, March 30, 2022, https://oceantomo.com/intangible-asset-market-value-study/.

Market Value of Ten Top Brands

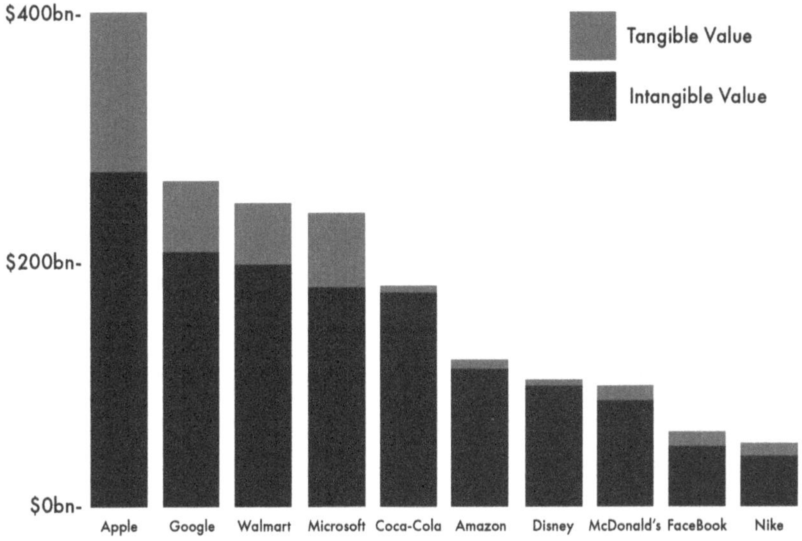

Source: "Business Owners, Are You Investing in the Right Places? Why You Should Manage Your Intangible Assets," My Asset Tag, n.d., https://www.myassettag.com/business-assets.

We are connected, inspired, and even defined by stories and intangible values. They give our lives meaning, purpose, and a deeper sense of belonging. This motivation can help decode why certain brands, whose market leaders have fused their brand identity with a shared intangible value woven together through emotionally compelling stories, are extraordinarily successful.

All around us, we can see the power of stories and enticing imagery, harnessed to clearly communicate shared intangible values. This is the language of human connection—ironically, one that is spoken universally but is taught nowhere until now, through the award-winning Intangience methodology[3] I developed that is used by major corporations and global brands.

I created this book to equip you with fluency in this language of connection because this is the language that can make the difference between the failure of a great product and the success of an ordinary one. It can even determine what gets you that job or promotion or the attention of someone you desire. It can help solve conflicts. It can influence behaviors for positive impact and greater purpose, and it can also help you spot manipulative practices, techniques, and devices.

We are connected, inspired, and even defined by stories and intangible values. They give our lives meaning, purpose, and a deeper sense of belonging.

We live in a world where there are more than seven thousand languages spoken and at a time when technology connects us better than ever and helps us translate much out of these linguistic differences. However, understanding a language is entirely different from identifying strongly with what is being shared.

This nuanced language of human connection is at the heart of some of the world's most successful brands and behind some of the world's most skilled communicators. You can describe this as the Currency of Connection or the Currency of Conversation in the way the message becomes highly shareable. This is determined by its relevance, the regard for the source through whom it was shared, and whether it resonated at a deeply, fundamentally important level with you.

The real-life stories contained here provide evidence for how we interpret the world and place value on things through the meaning we attribute to them. Throughout my career in branding across all industries and sectors, I learned to spot a pattern that repeats itself.

3 Visit Intangience.com to dive deeper into the Intangience methodology.

This insight gave me the ability, to a certain degree, to predict and ignite consumer and market responses. It would become the basis for the Intangience methodology.

Intangience comprises three schools of thought, each with three pathways or principles that guide you through the process of achieving breakthrough thinking on how to redefine your message to achieve authentic, meaningful connection and impressive results.

THE INTANGIENCE METHODOLOGY

Intangience is a portmanteau of the phrase *intangible* values and the *science* of human connection. It reveals what lies at the heart of agreement, empathy, and inspired conviction.

There are three foundational elements to Intangience, which we'll explore in greater detail in this book:

1. Pillars of Purpose: This approach goes beyond the usual brand-building architecture. It is a unique, introspective process that seeks the answers to three questions developed from the audience's perspective. The emerging insight will transform the way you see a challenge and how best to create a meaningful, resonant message.
2. Currency of Conversation: To inspire people to talk about a brand and share its message, the brand story must be relevant, it must originate from a highly regarded source or community, and the message must resonate at a deeply, fundamentally important level. The three principles identified here will reveal how to create brand popularity with a highly shareable message.
3. Science of Human Connection: Creating lasting, meaningful, emotional connection depends on your ability to inspire

> a passionate following, identifying the intangible value that fully represents your brand, and predicting both current and emerging trends that will influence consumer behavior.

There are specific techniques and devices that you can deploy that comprise the science behind it all. You will discover what these are and see how they are being used today by some of the best communicators and brands.

This methodology represents the markers of a journey—a journey that leads you from a thoughtful understanding of a brand's identity to determining the value of the currency around the brand's reputation and popularity, culminating in actions to ensure that the brand creates lasting, meaningful emotional connections with consumers.

At first, my motivation in identifying and developing the Intangience methodology was to create a powerful personal development program based upon my huge success in advertising and how the methodology I developed there worked in transforming ordinary brands into magical encounters. Intangience was born out of my need to show how the methodology of branding can be brought to bear in one's personal life.

I soon learned that people were more interested in using it for their business and branding development. So, I circled back to the world of advertising, where my agency had an impressive record of more than five hundred ADDY Awards and where my methodology was acclaimed by Harvard professors and corporate leaders. Ironically, while the business application of Intangience was the lure, it was impossible not to be personally impacted by the thinking and strategies of Intangience.

During my decades at the helm of my branding and advertising agency Ross | ReThink, I saw, again and again, how intangible values were at the heart of emotional connections with consumers, regardless of culture or country. I recognized that too many struggling brands had failed to understand that functionality and utilitarian purpose were not the only drivers of success. In fact, it was quite often the case that large successful brands didn't provide the best quality of offerings, yet they competed successfully to own market share against their competitors.

I discovered that what a brand means to consumers often counts more than the benefit it delivers to them. In much the same way that we mean more to people based on who we are rather than only what we provide, a brand's meaning to a loyal consumer is shaped through a shared intangible value embodied in that brand of choice.

They feel that the brand truly represents them.

As I've witnessed its impact, I've recognized that this methodology can do more than transform a global brand and accelerate its profitability. The Intangience methodology can create greater opportunities for all of us to connect our story with these intangible values, to recognize what truly shapes opinions, beliefs, feelings, and decisions, and to use that knowledge to communicate a message in a way that will resonate with every audience. It's a revolutionary philosophy that can and should be used by purpose-driven organizations and NGOs to equip them with a deeper understanding of the power of connection to influence behaviors for positive outcomes. That's why this methodology has been validated by the University for Peace established by the UN General Assembly through its Centre for Executive Education, and why the certificate course of study has been taken by thousands of global entrepreneurs, leaders, and business organizations.

In this book, I'll share the strategies that are at the heart of hundreds of international, award-winning campaigns. I'll explain how building fluency in the language of human connection launched a political movement that elevated a nation's first female prime minister, redefined a border dispute, quelled gang violence in a high-risk community, and created a collective identity for thirteen Caribbean island nations in a way no formal regional organization had ever achieved.

I'll also share a bit of my own journey from a childhood struggling to survive in a despotic dictatorship to a career of influence with global leaders and the creation of national and global initiatives centered around happiness and kindness.

This book is not intended to be a static resource—although I hope that you'll find its contents practical and applicable, whether your goal is to tell your own personal brand story more effectively or to elevate an individual or a product or service in a powerful, meaningful way. Consider this your invitation to join me in the purposeful work of what my friend, former Harvard professor and best-selling author Dr. Tal Ben-Shahar,[4] describes as "doing well and doing good." You'll find opportunities to assess insights, complete challenges, and identify how to apply your new understanding to your unique goals. Every chapter will start with a story because I believe in the power of compelling storytelling as the clearest demonstration of the Intangience methodology.

A great story can transform your perspective. It can create emotional connections that transcend borders and cultures. My hope is that this book will inspire you to think differently about the power of connection to create messages that resonate and spark positive change.

Now for a story about the language that the entire world speaks but hasn't been given the opportunity to effectively learn, until now.

Intangience. The Science of Human Connection. Let me tell you its story.

---

4 Learn more about Dr. Tal Ben-Shahar and his fascinating work at https://talben-shahar.com/

CHAPTER ONE

HOW TO SURVIVE IN A COUNTRY WHERE EATING BREAD IS ILLEGAL

I can see none of you are smugglers, that's why it is so loud.

—EUGENE ORMANDY[5]

As an eighteen-year-old amateur smuggler, I had one thought as we neared the police roadblock ahead: *Don't get caught.*

We were just three cars from the checkpoint, awaiting our turn, and every one of us was sweating nervously.

It had been a challenging journey, bumping along for more than two hours in the sweltering heat from Guyana's heartland, the county of Berbice, west to Georgetown, the capital city. Located on the Atlantic coast, Guyana neighbors both Brazil and Venezuela and is the only English-speaking country in South America.

It was also my home.

The police checkpoints were set up to hunt for contraband goods. Many items were considered contraband under the despotic

5 Eugene Ormandy quotations collected by members of the Philadelphia Orchestra, https://www.public.asu.edu/~schuring/Misc./Ormandy.html.

rule of Guyana's self-proclaimed "Comrade Leader," Linden Forbes Sampson Burnham, who had claimed power as the head of government when Guyana achieved independence from the British in 1966 (and who would not release it until his death in 1985). In a misguided effort he claimed was necessary to achieve economic independence, Burnham banned the import of food items that were part of our daily diet, including canned fish, fruit, split peas, cooking oil, and wheat flour.

It was the last prohibited item that was the source of my anxiety—because in the trunk of our car was a sack of that very illegal wheat flour. If the vehicle was searched, we were in serious trouble. The flour would indeed be confiscated, but that was only the beginning. We would be charged with criminal activity, arrested, and jailed.

Not every smuggler faced this terrifying fate. With enough money, you could bribe your way through the checkpoint. You could also escape arrest if you could produce a card identifying you as a member of Burnham's ruling political party, the People's National Congress.

Clearly, we were amateur smugglers, as no one in our group had a party card or sufficient funds to bribe our way out of arrest. In panicked whispers, we began to suggest potential explanations for why we were transporting the illegal flour. *We can say that we're taking the flour to the army headquarters*, someone suggested. *We need the flour to prepare a cook-up for a well-known political figure*, someone else muttered.

Too soon, we reached the head of the line. It was now our turn to be checked. The officer leaned into the trunk of our car and, with barely disguised delight, immediately spotted the contraband.

"This isn't my sack of flour," I said with a sudden rush of words.

He laughed sarcastically.

"It belongs to you … and me," I clarified.

"What are you telling me, Comrade?" he snapped menacingly.

I took a deep breath. "We have to learn to share in this country."

I pointed to the sack of flour. "This can't be all mine. There is enough to share with you and your colleagues."

The police officer broke into a smile and walked briskly back to his colleagues. After a moment of discussion, they directed me to drive the vehicle to another spot behind the barrier. They then proceeded to empty more than half of the sack into buckets and sent me on my way with a much lighter sack and a caution that, next time, things wouldn't be so easy. As we drove off, I didn't realize that this was just the beginning of the horror story that would ultimately inspire me to escape the tyranny of Burnham's Guyana.

It was also the beginning of another understanding—one that would shape my future career. Because in that impoverished country, behind the harrowing experiences of risking my life for a bit of flour or a tiny jar of cooking oil was a deeper lesson in how the world trades and the messages that connect us.

Scarcity Value

Guyana was a country where, if you saw a long line outside a store, you would join it without asking questions. That line meant that something scarce was suddenly available. It didn't matter whether you needed or wanted what was being sold. Its mere availability meant that it was valuable, and someone would be willing to pay well for it.

Let me pause my story to ask you a relevant question, one that connects this bit of history with the present: Have you seen the red velvet ropes attached to poles outside luxury brand stores today?

Lines of customers form, sometimes as far as around the corner of the establishment, waiting to be allowed in to spend huge sums of money on the costly items offered inside. But often, if you're lucky enough to be able to peek inside the store, you'll see … very few customers. Those ropes and poles aren't designed for effective crowd control. They are part of a scarcity value technique deployed to create precious demand for the luxury brand.

It was British economist Lionel Robbins who first connected scarcity to economic value. A famous cookie jar experiment by a team of American researchers built on his theory, demonstrating that when objects are considered to be scarce (in that case, when there were fewer cookies in a cookie jar), they are identified as being more valuable and desirable, without a single cookie being tasted.[6]

SCARCITY VALUE

6 Stephen Worchel et al., "Effects of Supply and Demand on Ratings of Object Value," *Journal of Personality and Social Psychology* 32, no. 5 (1975): 906–14, https://www.doi.org/10.1037/0022-3514.32.5.906.

A sense of scarcity suggests that something is valuable. That's why lining up for access is part of a luxury brand's art of creating an experience of exclusivity and status. There are many articles and research papers that have been written on the psychology of queuing up as used by luxury retailers.[7] But for now, imagine seeing this experience today from the perspective gleaned earlier in my life.

In Guyana, there were professional *liners*—people whose job it was to occupy a spot in a line. These liners might queue up outside the US Embassy, for example, very early in the day and then sell that place to you. The further up the line, of course, the more you would pay the liner who had waited to earn that spot.

Let's return to the scarcity value idea and its connection to luxury—in this case, to the luxury brand Louis Vuitton. What do you think Louis Vuitton does with all its unsold merchandise?

It destroys every item that remains unsold in order to retain its exclusivity.

Rather than selling unsold bags at a discount, Louis Vuitton is laser-focused on reinforcing its brand message of prestige and rarity. As a result, the worth of the bags—that is, what people are willing to pay for them—is higher. It's not just the quality and craftsmanship that give the Louis Vuitton brand its worth. It is the intangible value developed by understanding the techniques that embody the brand name, connecting the Louis Vuitton logo to luxury and exclusivity, reserved for the privileged few. Creating queues outside stores is simply one manipulative device among many other brand development strategies.

---

7 Anita Radón, "Luxury Brand Exclusivity Strategies – An Illustration of a Cultural Collaboration," *Journal of Business Administration Research* 1, no. 1 (2012): 6–110, https://www.doi.org/10.5430/jbar.v1n1p106.

Where I grew up, needs were much more basic. Our "luxury" items were potatoes and sardines, and most Guyanese were forced to engage in some form of smuggling to acquire them. Even cigarettes were sold not by the packet but singly.

While some items were indeed necessary, such as bread, others had local replacements when they became too scarce. As an example, apples could be exchanged for any of the many other delicious fruits grown in the country, and cassava could replace potatoes. But the fact that these ordinary items could be deemed a luxury, available only for the privileged, was my early lesson in how human behavior drives desirability.

It all lands on a simple principle that determines everything in our lives: meaning.

Something only has value when it holds meaning for someone.

The extent to which people will go to acquire something they want and the amount they are willing to pay for it are inherently built into identifying what *meaning* the object of desire holds for them.

Something only has value when it holds meaning for someone.

During my childhood and teen years in Guyana, people risked their safety and freedom for a bunch of grapes because their unavailability made them even more desirable. They were not quite literally priceless, but those grapes were intensely desirable in part because of the high price you might pay to acquire them.

It wasn't the taste or the nutritional value of the grapes that created the demand. It was the intangible value of scarcity that made them so precious and desirable.

Whether we're talking about prohibited grapes or Louis Vuitton bags, the intangible value of desirability is often punctuated by the scarce supply that gives it a meaning and, in turn, a value and worth not determined by utilitarian purpose or use.

But if value is determined by meaning, what creates worth? By worth, I'm thinking of what the market is willing to pay for something. *Worth is, in fact, determined by the extent to which someone believes in the value of an object*, and that ultimately completes the Circle of Consumer Sentiment, bringing it back to *meaning*.

The Circle of Consumer Sentiment

Let's make sure that we clearly define some vocabulary that is important for the language of connection.

Value is established through the meaning that consumers attach to something. Worth is determined by what the market is willing to pay for something. The extent to which a consumer *believes* in the value, in turn, establishes what anything is *worth*.

It wasn't the taste or the nutritional value of the grapes that created the demand. It was the intangible value of scarcity that made them so precious and desirable.

This is what creates the Circle of Consumer Sentiment and explains how it leads back to meaning.

But the Science of Human Connection doesn't end there. In fact, that is just the beginning of understanding the patterns of our behavior when it comes to worth, value, and scarcity.

There is a process to it all—a process that the Intangience methodology helps us to understand through three unique schools of thought, which will be revealed during the course of each chapter throughout this book, both for your awareness and application.

May you use this knowledge wisely and always to serve a greater purpose.

Now, to conclude my bread smuggling story, I share this brief account of what finally nudged me to not simply leave Guyana but to escape it.

My neighbor, a baker from the island of Barbados, used to bake small amounts of bread and pastries to sell in the neighborhood. These banned items, prepared with contraband flour, could be delivered only at night under the cloak of darkness. Most of the country rarely had electric power because of the dilapidated infrastructure, so light at night was mostly provided by candles and kerosene lamps or, for those who were more fortunate, small generators.

It was on one of those dark nights, as my brave neighborhood baker was handing me the much-sought-after, rare, hugely expensive package of delicacies of bread and pastries, that we heard the sound of a police siren in the distance. Poor Baj, as he was known, dropped the package and ran, leaving the bread and pastries scattered all over the ground.

No police arrived, but the incident had a significant effect on me. I realized, yet again, that I could actually have been arrested for the "crime" of buying bread!

The next morning, I grimaced when I saw a government banner overhead, which read, "Feed, Clothe and House the Nation by 1976." That message was a mockery of a country that was undernourished, lacking basic freedoms, and largely homeless. I knew that I had to escape my birthplace.

Propagandist Thinking Versus Poignant Thinking

An important lesson gleaned from these experiences was the difference between propagandist and poignant thinking in communication.

The government of the day controlled more than 80 percent of the economy and the few media channels available. No foreign magazines or other printed materials were allowed in. The transmission signals of foreign radio stations were reportedly jammed. The government managed everything we read, saw, or heard. Yet, despite this absolute control, their messages failed to resonate.

You don't need to live under a dictatorial political system in order to find examples of this type of propagandist messaging. It is in clear evidence around us all of the time. Much of the advertising, branding, and communication we see is propagandist rather than poignant in nature.

You can buy all of the media time possible, but unless you create resonance, it means nothing and convinces no one.

You can buy all of the media time possible, but unless you create resonance, it means nothing and convinces no one.

There is a cartoon I came across that depicts this so well. It features a turkey with a wooden leg holding a drumstick. He's clearly been chomping away at the drumstick and confidently declares, "I am delicious!"

Illustration used with permission from Jim Benton ©JimBenton.com

It is the perfect illustration of the cannibalism of a message through what is clearly a self-destructive process. The only person actually consuming the message, to their own detriment, is the one who owns it.

It's the reason I say, as an advertising man myself, that ads that clearly appear as ads do not work. In nearly every case, the moment they are recognized as ads, they have already failed. What's required is authentic engagement. Don't attempt to just persuade. Create meaningful connections.

Understanding what the consumer's intangible values are and how to weave a compelling story that emotionally connects and resonates is the way to develop poignancy.

When your brand genuinely embodies those shared, *intangible* values deemed important to the particular consumer you seek to attract, you then have a foundation upon which you can create authenticity and resonance in your messaging.

Consider this: It costs nearly $14 million for a sixty-second commercial that airs during the Super Bowl. Yet I can show you an ad for Dove that ran for about fifty-eight seconds without revealing anything of its offering. The story told is emotionally charged and moving—though in fact, the product never appears at all. But in the final few seconds of the ad, the logo of the brand was revealed, subtly linking the intangible value communicated in the ad with the brand story.[8]

It is impossible to guess the product (unless you're clairvoyant!), but that's not the purpose of this exercise. The brand identity's intangible values are embodied in the story. Further, the brand validates its message by creating a global movement around the intangible values inherent in the brand message.

This is what I mean by the power of poignant rather than propagandist messages. The brand's intangible values are embodied and communicated through an emotionally compelling story. No imposed, self-absorbed, dictatorially induced perspective tells us how to connect.

Imagine being the brand owner who is investing millions of dollars for a single minute of exposure, and the agency brings you a TV spot that *never* shows your product or service being used or even spoken aloud!

I've been in those meetings and have had many executives dictate to me what they feel would best communicate their brand through utilitarian purpose or benefit. But that is not how great brands are built, nor is it the way to create global movements.

---

8 "Celebrating Father's Day with Dads Who Care | Dove Men+Care," YouTube, 2015, https://youtu.be/QoqWo3SJ73c.

Developing the language of human connection requires what could be defined as the absence of ego in the presence of humility—a willingness to understand the hearts and minds of your audience and to share a story that matters most to them *emotionally*. It is the difference between perspective and perception. It is easy for each of us to see the world through our own eyes and experiences, but to perceive reality through the eyes of *someone else* is the most powerful way to truly understand others and to know how to create authentic connection.

Escape to the Next Chapter

Let me return one last time to my childhood home and my decision to flee.

I had managed to scrape together enough money for a flight out of Guyana. I arrived at the airport's departure lounge with no money—in part because I had used my scarce funds to pay for the flight and in part because, even if I had more, the government didn't allow anyone to leave the country with any of its scarce foreign currency.

I sat in the lounge, alone and wondering what my life would become. I felt as though it couldn't get any worse than the risk of being jailed for eating bread.

I thought about a handmade sign I had seen on the road just outside the airport. The message seemed appropriate:

"*Will the last one to leave kindly blow out the candle.*"

Little did I know then that the message in that simple sign would one day spark the launch of the first and most historic political campaign of its kind in the region—one that would be the catalyst for transformation in political communication. It would trigger the return of democracy to Guyana and enable the election of the first US-born female president of a country.

And I would be thrust into becoming that campaign's creator. But that's another story ...

Intangience Insights

Consider this Intangience insight: Something only has value when it holds meaning for those who seek to possess it.

Think of anything of value in life. Whether it is a physical asset, investment instrument, or human relationship, its value is determined by the *meaning* attributed to it.

Beyond utilitarian purpose and functionality lie a whole realm of connections people will form in the desirability, pursuit, and acquisition of something based upon how much it means to them. It is in this world of intangible values that meaning is found and the value and worth of a brand emerge.

Something only has value when it holds meaning for those who seek to possess it.

Just as in branding, this insight applies to your personal life: When you find meaning in any area of your life, purpose emerges, and, in turn, authentic happiness is discovered. In contrast, if your very life has no meaning, then it is of little value.

Intangience Inquiries

1. Why were Guyanese willing to risk so much to acquire expensive prohibited items, such as grapes, when there were local alternatives?
2. What technique do some luxury retailers use to reinforce their exclusivity?

3. What establishes value for anything?
4. Why don't ads work?
5. What distinguishes perspective from perception?

CHAPTER TWO

HOW TO SELL USED TOOTHBRUSHES

We have become second-hand human beings...

—JIDDU KRISHNAMURTI

Early in my career, I successfully sold used toothbrushes.

There's a specific art to selling a used toothbrush. It's relatively easy to find customers eager to buy a used car, a vintage item of clothing, or an apartment that served as a home to previous tenants. But a used toothbrush? That requires a unique sales approach.

Imagine a slick salesman rapping on your door or approaching you on the street, offering up a used toothbrush for sale. This concept was the inspiration for a highly successful ad campaign that I ran many decades ago, before the internet, before social media. My goal was to create what we now call a viral message—a message that would be liked and shared in an analog way.

I wanted this campaign to be memorable and become what Seth Godin calls "remarkable"[9] (having the ability to be remarked upon).

One of the key principles of Intangience is what I call the Currency of Conversation or the Currency of Connection. There are three principles that guide a shareable story: relevance, regard, and resonance.

In order to inspire people to talk about anything and be inspired to share it, that story or message must first be *relevant*. It must then come from a source, spokesperson, or community held in high *regard*. Finally, the message must *resonate* at a deep, fundamentally important level. We'll talk more about this principle and how to practice it throughout this book. For now, I invite you to consider how each of those three elements (relevance, regard, and resonance) propelled a brand into something that everyone talked about.

A series of ads that ran through a national radio *and* print campaign featured slick salesmen, and their pitch was for used toothbrushes as items of significant use and value—things they claimed every buyer wanted and needed.

---

9 Seth Godin, *Purple Cow: Transform Your Business by Being Remarkable* (Portfolio Books, 2003).

Examine the bristles of this fine used toothbrush now on sale and you'll find you can still get a lot more out of it. Consider the fact that it's being sold for a quarter of the price of a new one and you'll also discover it's a bargain you can't afford to miss.

Well, we knew you wouldn't buy that. Yet it's exactly what you do when choosing a used auto part without knowing who's been using it, even the way in which it's been used or whether it's safe at all! You'll agree -it's a risk of money and life. Be sensible. You wouldn't buy used toothbrushes; don't buy used auto parts.

Choose new genuine Nissan parts.

Almost overnight, the campaign created a buzz. The exaggerated attempt to sell something so absurd caught everyone's attention. The campaign was so successful that we expanded it into a series of ads. There were salesmen selling used razor blades and salesmen selling used light bulbs. What was behind all of this?

The campaign's inspiration came from a challenge Nissan was facing in the Caribbean. Used auto parts dealers were selling cheap, unauthorized, and unsafe car parts and convincing customers through what were called "under the mango tree mechanic shops" (inexpensive mechanics who set up a makeshift repair operation under a proverbial tree). They claimed that these used auto parts were good to use as replacements. While it was all illegal, the black market for these parts and their use in repairs was impacting the Nissan parts division's ability to safely repair cars while also eluding the authorities' ability to stamp out the trade. Warnings and advisories were not working.

But within a few months of the used toothbrush, used razor blades, and used light bulbs ads appearing, Nissan had edged back to reclaim its market.

Why was the used toothbrush campaign successful in a way that Nissan's previous attempts had not been? Their earlier messages had focused on the obvious logic of the safety and dependability of using only new, authorized Nissan parts. It was too cerebral to be truly persuasive. There was neither an emotional connection nor a compelling story that everyone could agree upon and find interesting enough to share. By dramatizing the idea of buying a used auto part to be as ridiculous as buying a used toothbrush, we were able to more clearly link the idea of *used* to undesirable and ineffective.

The other obvious ploy, of course, was the use of humor to show the absurdity of a behavior that, if otherwise addressed, might easily be rejected. Humor allowed the audience to laugh at themselves and open their minds to entertaining the message that there was no way for anyone to determine either how good or safe a used auto part would be.

For the Nissan auto parts division, reclaiming its value was achieved by redefining the meaning customers linked to a used part. Now, customers associated these parts with something cheap and unsafe. The creative device of a used toothbrush to convey the message is what the Intangience methodology describes as derivative meaning.

Derivative Meaning

Derivative meaning is a concept I have developed to further define features such as brand equity and worth. It's the point at which things assume a larger value and worth beyond function, logic, and rationality.

The lessons I learned from the used toothbrush campaign were so impactful that I actually developed it into an exercise in my Intangience workshops. It never fails to challenge any participant, no matter where in the world I conduct the sessions.

In my master class, I hand out an assortment of used toothbrushes and ask the participants to consider what value could be imbued to a used toothbrush in its present state. They are then required to sell the used toothbrush. The caveat is that it can only be presented as a toothbrush. It cannot be repurposed in another way, such as to clean something else.

Thus, it presents a challenge.

I invite you to try this exercise yourself.

Consider how you might sell a used toothbrush.

What would your pitch be?

What intangible value could the used toothbrush embody, and what emotionally compelling story could be told about it?

As you'll see, this is a disruptive exercise that requires you to move beyond your natural inclination to consider a nonfunctional purpose for a used toothbrush. It reinforces the derivative meaning that a brand's defined intangible value can hold and where its true worth often emerges. This is not to say utilitarian purpose isn't a key consideration, but emotional connections and consumer-driven considerations are much more complex than the weight of quality and function. *Meaning* drives that evaluation process.

The used toothbrush exercise nudges you to think of ways in which you can develop a different meaning that the toothbrush might hold for the consumer. In one of my master class sessions, a group of participants created a story presenting the toothbrush as a symbol of the movement against the trafficking of young women. The toothbrush used during the months of a particular young victim's captivity became a symbol of a campaign shining a spotlight on young women being exploited and viewed as unworthy of any human value.

These participants developed an emotional story of a young Venezuelan girl who was kidnapped and trafficked. Abused and used in the worst ways imaginable, she was one of the fortunate ones who escaped. The toothbrush given to her was what she used during the months of her captivity. She would later launch a campaign to highlight the plight of young girls and women like her. The used toothbrush became the symbol of the campaign. Funds from those contributing to "buying" the used toothbrush went toward a foundation dedicated to rescuing others.

This make-believe story created by the participants demonstrated their ability to have the used toothbrush assume a meaning and therefore a value and worth. There was no attempt to sell its function, but instead, an intangible value was embodied in the used toothbrush. The story made many in the room emotional.

The used toothbrush and what it symbolized and meant to those who identified with the cause, in effect, created value and worth. In this example, the offering was stripped of functionality, and the derivative meaning became the persuasive device.

May you remember these principles each time you brush your teeth.

Want to Buy a Bottle of Air?

I used to love watching a particular episode of *Sesame Street* in which a dodgy character called Lefty sells Ernie (yes, my namesake) a bottle of air. He makes the point that he isn't selling the *bottle*. He's selling what's *in* it. Each time Ernie says, "Air?" Lefty says, "Shhh!" and looks around guardedly. He explains to Ernie that air is so important. We can't breathe without it. Lefty even demonstrates to Ernie that his harmonica needs air to make a sound, and a balloon needs air if it's not to remain deflated. He concludes with this pitch: "So, with the air in this bottle, you can breathe, you can play music, you can blow up a balloon!"

Lefty then convinces Ernie to buy the air inside the bottle, but *not* the bottle, for "just" five cents!

I've never forgotten the lessons from this enjoyable bit of satire. I saw it as a wonderful way of understanding how we can reframe a sales pitch on just about anything.

Here is an interesting question for you: What product is available for free in most parts of the world, yet consumers are willing to pay for it, and there are more than one thousand brands vying for a share of this multibillion-dollar market? Pause to reflect on the answer before reading on.

Growing up in one of the poorest countries in the Western Hemisphere, I understood better than most the value of recycled, reconstructed, and repurposed items. Even ice cream cups became the housing that held a locally assembled vehicle's signal bulbs, as there were no replacements. With that same make-do spirit, people were pressed into trying to make bread out of rice flour.

So, it's no stretch that clear, potable water was not taken for granted. There is, in fact, a funny story that illustrates this well, which would later unwittingly help me develop what I regard as a convincing branding exercise for water that powerfully demonstrates how applying the Intangience methodology works in sixty seconds! More on that later—but first, this hilarious encounter.

My stepfather had invited some friends over from Trinidad on a hunting trip into Guyana's fascinating forested areas. Arriving in Georgetown, they made certain assumptions that no Guyanese ever would in those days, such as when you turned on a tap, you could expect clean, clear potable water.

You can imagine their shock and surprise upon seeing brown water chug out of the tap and finding a small, gray-colored guppy swimming in the glass.

"Oh shit!" one of the Trinidadian guys exclaimed. "The water is brown, and there is a fish in my glass!"

Calmly, my stepdad, Tony, asked, "Is it alive?"

"Yes, it's alive! Look at it!" his friend shouted in disbelief as he held up the glass of muddy water with the fish wriggling around in it.

"Then it's OK," my stepdad replied. "If the fish is alive, that means the water is drinkable."

"What?" The Trinidadian visitor was still reeling from the shock of all of this and missing the irony of the humor.

"In Guyana, we don't have enough chemicals to purify and clear the water," my stepdad explained, "so the government puts these little ugly guppies in the water system to help show us whether the tap water is safe."

The room exploded with laughter. Truth be told, the water mains were so rusted that fish from the trenches often leaked into the water supply system.

Against this background of the urgent need for water, I found it very amusing later in life to discover that there are more than one thousand brands of water vying for a share of a multibillion-dollar market. This is well documented in Youngme Moon's fascinating book, *Different.*[10]

In the book, Youngme Moon explains how research has shown that consumers can't differentiate the taste between one brand of water and the next, yet these brands go to extreme lengths to identify

10 Youngme Moon, *Different: Escaping the Competitive Herd* (Crown Business, 2011).

their difference. The ad copy quoted by the author demonstrates how ridiculous these brands' claims are. There are even brands with names such as Bling H2O, which carry a price tag of as much as $70 a bottle in Las Vegas nightclubs. On a visit to a five-star hotel in Miami, I discovered an offering in my room of a water brand called Nevas, which was packaged like a bottle of champagne for the startling price of $85. It was actually cheaper to drink the champagne!

Used toothbrushes, bottles of air, even $85 bottles of water—the true worth of each of these items depends far less on their utilitarian purpose and far more on their intangible value. The emotional connection attached to each one depends on the stories that are told, which inspire you to view them in a very different light.

Later in the book, after you are introduced to the three schools of thought on Intangience, you will see how an imaginary brand of simple, pure water—without special packaging or a price advantage—can be imbued with intangible value, allowing it to strongly resonate, credibly differentiate itself, be highly regarded, and command a higher price—even without live fish swimming in it!

Intangience Insights

The intangible value or *derivative meaning* embodied in a brand that is deemed highly important by the consumer is often more *persuasively important* than quality, utilitarian purpose, or functionality.

Brand value can rise and fall on this idea of derivative meaning and how effectively it is developed.

In much the same way that we often mean more to people than the things we provide, the same holds true for brand relationships.

Too often, business owners and brand managers get overly focused on the functionality considerations of a product or service.

Yes, of course, utilitarian purpose and quality considerations are important. The fundamentals of business always apply, but one cannot ignore or deny the compelling reasons consumers are often persuaded to choose one brand over another.

We are essentially sentient beings, not machines. Even in the face of the most compelling evidence, with all of the facts presented, we still may not be persuaded to change our decision or opinion simply because of how we *feel.*

The intangible value or *derivative meaning* embodied in a brand that is deemed highly important by the consumer is often more *persuasively important* than quality, utilitarian purpose, or functionality.

It's the reason so many of us choose to have a relationship with someone we know isn't right for us. We persist largely because of our feelings, not cerebral thinking or thoughtful analysis. Any brand that seeks to meaningfully connect with its audience must have its intangible value clearly identified—a value embodied in the brand that will resonate with the consumer. But it's more than simply identifying that value. You must then weave an emotionally compelling brand story around it.

Still, that is just the beginning. Those shared intangible values must be manifested through events and activities that bring them to life and validate the greater purpose seen to be held by the brand.

It's not enough to say, "This is what our brand values are." You must bring those values into being through authentic connection, just like the old adage, "To thine own self be true."[11]

11 William Shakespeare, "Act 1, Scene 3," Essay, In *Hamlet* (Yale University Press, 2003).

Intangience Inquiries

1. If you had to create a brand message that wasn't just about the utilitarian purpose of your product or service, what could the brand embody that powerfully and emotionally connects with your audience?
2. What was it about the used toothbrush ad campaign for Nissan that convinced consumers not to purchase used parts?
3. How would you sell a used toothbrush without repurposing it?
4. What intangible value could your brand of water have that would resonate?
5. What is derivative meaning?

INTANGIENC
INTANGIENC
INTANGIENC
INTANGIENC
INTANGIENC
INTANGIENC
INTANGIENC
INTANGIENC
INTANGIENC
INTANGIENC
INTANGIENC
INTANGIENC

CHAPTER THREE

HOW TO CREATE AN INSPIRING MOVEMENT

I am no longer accepting the things I cannot change. I am changing the things I cannot accept.

—ANGELA DAVIS

I am proudest of three things in my life, all connected to women's empowerment:

- Raising my daughter largely on my own as a single dad from the time she was a baby
- Being deeply involved in an election campaign that brought to power the first female president of Guyana (who happened to be born in the United States)
- Developing and managing almost every aspect of an election campaign that resulted in the first female prime minister of Trinidad and Tobago—truly an against-all-odds result

How Janet Rosenberg Jagan[12] became the first female US-born president of a nation is a fascinating story that requires a lot of reading on the history and political machinations of the period. Just to provide a quick perspective and understanding of why this unlikely event occurred, I must apologetically crunch decades of historical happenings into a few paragraphs. The focus here is not on the outcome of a single election campaign. It's on the principles that inspire others. It's on creating a message that inspires a national movement.

The Guyanese dictator Forbes Burnham died in 1985, and the reins of power in the Co-operative Republic of Guyana shifted to a self-proclaimed economic reformist called Desmond Hoyte. Hoyte used his predecessor's playbook and rigged an election to illegally gain office, and then deferred elections for a further two years after the expiration of his stolen term.

Finally, in 1992, Hoyte reluctantly agreed to hold Guyana's first internationally supervised general elections in decades. The country was destitute and in urgent need of foreign aid, but that aid was being withheld until free and fair elections were held. With the intervention of former US President Jimmy Carter and his renowned Carter Center, the integrity of the election process was assured. In that tense climate, a group of international election observers, including those from the Caribbean, began to arrive.

Despite the international oversight to ensure free and fair elections, President Hoyte was persuaded by a group of business people that he could be "reelected" (not that he was ever legitimately elected in the first place!). This group was called the Committee for the Reelection of the President (note the irony in the acronym CREEP). It was perhaps a sign of how tone-deaf the whole power structure was to public opinion and the way things were on the ground.

12 Read about Janet Jagan's incredible story at https://ianrandlepublishers.com/27634-2/.

Convinced that he could win in a fair election and pressured by Jimmy Carter's efforts to restore Guyana's standing as a globally recognized democratic state, Hoyte launched his reelection campaign.

At the time, I was no longer living in Guyana. I had moved to Trinidad and Tobago, and it was there that I happened upon Dr. Cheddi Jagan[13], former prime minister of what was then known as British Guiana. (He served in that post from 1961 to 1964.) Dr. Jagan was the current opposition leader and leader of the People's Progressive Party (PPP). I overheard him speaking on the phone at a hotel in Trinidad, asking for support for his presidential election campaign to unseat Desmond Hoyte and overcome the despotic rule Guyana had endured for decades.

In an ironic twist, Dr. Jagan had been removed from office through an intervention by the United Kingdom and the United States because of fear of his avowed socialist ideology. Now, three decades later, the United States (through the Carter Center) was attempting to right these wrongs. The Republic of Guyana, as it had become, was finally poised for its first internationally supervised elections.

I saw Dr. Jagan as a politician who had been denied power through corrupt means, collusion with external forces, and a collaboration of condonation by successive Caribbean leaders. His avowed socialist political beliefs were often offered up as the reason for the denial of his legitimate access to power and the allowance of the democratic will to prevail. This was despite the Burnham alternative being despotic rule, flagrant corruption, rampant nepotism, and open brutality. It was the most unjust of situations.

Dr. Jagan was a candidate for president, but it seemed that much of what had been promised to him by the local business community

13 Learn more about Dr. Cheddi Jagan and his inspiring journey at https://jagan.org/Biography/CJ%20Bio/cj_biography2.html.

prior to his arrival in Trinidad from Guyana wasn't materializing, and he had an election to mount. At the time, I had a small, fledgling creative shop with absolutely no experience in political work, but I offered to help Dr. Jagan and his PPP at no cost.

Little did I know then that it was to be the start of a long and highly successful career in political campaigning. It became a watershed election and one I developed in such a way that it redefined political campaigning and marketing.

It was also my first lesson in how intangible values are hugely important in developing a candidate's public profile.

What was Dr. Jagan's toughest challenge? To shake off the outdated label of being a socialist. His opponent, Desmond Hoyte, was claiming to be a reformer and was being credited with opening a free market economy. By contrast, Dr. Jagan was being described as a political dinosaur who would foist a failed socialist experiment on a beleaguered, poverty-stricken country where 95 percent of its GDP went to paying off its foreign debt.

This leads us to consider the answer to this question: What creates conviction?

In the last chapter, we considered that facts, no matter how heavily they are weighed in support of an argument, are less powerful than emotions. I can convince you of a fact, but you can still hold on to your position because of how you *feel* about any given matter. We see this well illustrated when it comes to matters such as religion and politics. Opinions on these things are driven by feelings or "faith" and any number of factors that may have little or nothing to do with intellectual reasoning.

They are often formed by important influences, such as ingrained beliefs, cultural identities, historical experiences, and, of course, traditional voting patterns.

While it might seem that any alternative to the failed administration of the time would be readily embraced, ethnic divisions in Guyana made the situation far more complex. The country also had a history of riots that first exposed deep racial tensions in the 1960s—events that older Guyanese mildly and curiously refer to as "the disturbances." Although Guyanese now integrate well as a multiethnic, multicultural society, these ethnic tensions continue to simmer, particularly in the political arena.

Earlier in the book, we explored how a brand's intangible values are embodied and communicated through an emotionally compelling story. In this context, we needed to create an authentic, poignant message for Dr. Jagan to ensure that voters understood his strength of character and integrity and what he represented through the years in his courageous struggle to return Guyana to democracy. We persuaded him (despite his strong protests) to wear a jacket and tie rather than a shirt jacket for TV appearances and to refine his more aggressive nonverbal mannerisms when emphatically making a point. The message that we crafted—the *brand* we developed for Dr. Jagan—centered around the idea of unity and optimism. Guyana was a country divided by politics, ethnicity, and economic disparities. I quickly discovered that what worked well in creating a consensus among the divided population was less logical political messaging and more emotionally charged content.

The Candle

You might recall, at the end of chapter 1, my spotting the sign near the airport that said so much about life in Guyana in the early 1980s: "Will the last one to leave kindly blow out the candle."

That sign was the inspiration for one of the more memorable ads created for the PPP election campaign. I realized that what the campaign required was a device that would cut across all boundaries. A single resonant message that could be a consensus point for all Guyanese, irrespective of where they were from or what ethnicity they happened to be. I found it in the candle.

The candle represented the decadence and broken infrastructure of a failed political system foisted upon Guyanese, who were forced to light candles or kerosene lamps for light at night. Load shedding, as it was called, simply meant that there would sometimes be days with no electrical power. When it was available, it came in fluctuating surges for a few scarce hours.

Everyone was affected by this. For many people, their only reliable source of light was a candle. It was the great equalizer I needed. The absence of a reliable electrical supply was a burden endured across the length and breadth of the impoverished nation. Even though, by the time elections were due, the power grid had improved somewhat and there was a slight increase in the supply, it was far from reliable or regular.

I produced a thirty-second black-and-white TV ad that simply showed a candle melting. In those days, there was no time-lapse technology available, so we had to shoot in real time and edit the effect of the melting moments. The only audio was that of a clock ticking. Eventually, the candle melted away into a swirl of smoke with the words, "Time's up, Desmond" (an obvious reference to then-president Desmond Hoyte).

The impact of the ad was beyond what I expected. The resonance of this simple visual reference rippled across Guyana and became a talking point everywhere. The reason could be found in the readily relatable experience of Guyanese suffering in silence and darkness for such a long time. The absence of a voice-over allowed the viewer to experience the message at a visceral level. The unexpected melting of the candle, revealing a cryptic message signaling that the time had come for the administration to end, elicited a shared response from Guyanese of all walks of life.

Every time there was a cut in electricity, day or night, people would invoke the phrase. Each time the ad ran, people would give voice to the end, saying aloud, "Time's up, Desmond!" It became a rallying cry across the nation, with everyone united by that singular message.

Relevance, Regard, Resonance

While the stories in this chapter cover the restoration of democracy to a country after three decades and, as you'll see next, the election of the first US-born female president, the election of the youngest head of state in the world, and the election of the first female prime minister of an island nation, my purpose isn't to shift your focus to the historical political situations described. Instead, I want you to think about how this was all achieved through understanding and applying the Intangience principles. These stories are intended to inspire you to recognize that it's possible to create a movement around shared intangible values that can break through tribal and other differences to create overwhelming support for a new idea, a new action, or, as in this example, a national movement for democracy.

I have found that the thing that ignites voters most in many political campaigns is when a core message hits a common chord and universally affects everyone at an *emotional* level. Here is an interesting question for you, regardless of which political candidate or party you supported during the 2016 US presidential campaigns of Donald Trump and Hillary Clinton.

What was Trump's campaign slogan?

Even today, many years after that campaign was first launched, most Americans can readily identify the slogan "Make America Great Again."

But if I ask even the most die-hard Democratic supporters to identify Hillary Clinton's campaign slogan, almost no one can recall it. Can you?

If you cannot, consider this fact: Trump's campaign committee spent about $238.9 million through mid-October 2016 compared with $450.6 million by Clinton's. While I understand that there were other factors, such as where the funds were deployed and how much free media Trump gained with his outlandish messaging and controversial style, one still has to find it remarkable that, with so much invested everywhere to blast the Clinton theme, few can recall it. The Clinton slogan was plastered on banners, podiums, billboards, and placards at rallies, and it was seen in print and on TV. But it is rarely remembered.

Her slogan was, "Stronger Together."

I recount this here only to reinforce the importance of the language of connection—of resonance when it comes to communication. This isn't just true of political campaigns. It's true for any form of messaging.

It's why I refer to Intangience as the language of human connection.

I mentioned earlier that there are more than seven thousand languages spoken in the world. Even if you're a polyglot, you may be able to communicate effectively but still fail to create an authentic connection and bridge real understanding. You might as well be speaking a whole other language, such is the dissonance.

In the Guyana election scenario, the facts were clearly there. There was an internationally recognized need to have a change of government by the ballot after decades of being ruled by the bullet of a dictatorship.

But all kinds of things get in the way of such clarity: tribalism, ethnic insecurities, religious beliefs, culture, and even education. The challenge was (to coin a phrase) to get them to "*see* what you *mean*."

There were, of course, several other techniques and strategies used in that election campaign that would capture the imagination of the electorate. While it was always expected that Dr. Jagan and his party would win any free and fair election, it also had to be *free from fear*. Supporters of the PPP had to feel free to vote, despite the fear inspired by years of subjugation. The people also needed to feel confident that the results would be certain and that the ruling party's supporters wouldn't respond to a narrow loss with riots and other acts of violence.

My aim was to create a campaign that would overwhelm anything the ruling party could muster up. It wasn't enough for Dr. Jagan to win at the polling booth on election day. He had to create the widespread expectation that he was the clear winner. We did this not only through a series of memorable ads but also through infectious campaign songs with a fusion of African and Indian rhythms, all rolling out faster than the opposite side could form a reply.

The campaign left the sitting government in its wake. It succeeded in making the PPP seem modern and relevant, despite attempts by the ruling party to instill fear through repeated charges that Dr. Jagan would propel the country into Communist chaos.

The irony was that I mounted the first American-style political ad campaign ever seen in the Caribbean region for what was traditionally perceived as a very socialist party.

It was a full multimedia campaign with billboards, radio, print, and TV spots, and all the political campaign paraphernalia.

It took the country by storm through the sheer weight and imagination of it. While the PPP looked modern, progressive, and ready for office, the ruling party was left in its tracks, looking outdated and outmaneuvered.

They tried responding with attempts to remake Desmond Hoyte as a leader with an economic recovery program that was liberalizing the economy and making available items that hadn't been seen for sale in decades (albeit at exorbitant prices). We responded with an ad that likened this to someone who cruelly amputates your legs and then offers you crutches to hobble around while expecting you to continually express your gratitude.

In another TV ad, a hand attempted to erase a list of the miserable past events Guyana's citizens had been forced to endure, only to see the words reappearing as a voice-over described Desmond Hoyte's futile attempt to erase his past and the impact of what he had done to the country.

I also used humor, such as a TV ad that featured a close-up of a young boy fishing with a rod in what appeared to be a large pond. As the camera zoomed out, it revealed that he was actually fishing in a huge, gaping pothole on a roadway—one of the many craters cluttering the country's dismally deteriorated roadways!

The takeaway from all of this was the style in which the political points were scored. With the facts being obvious, it's tempting to simply state them and expect everyone to agree. But it doesn't quite work that way in the court of public opinion.

One of the key principles of Intangience in this regard is what I call the Currency of Conversation. I've mentioned this earlier, but now let's spend time considering the way in which this Currency of Conversation, a highly shareable message, is created.

If you encounter something that really resonates, you're very likely to share it with others. This is true of a message, a movie, a book, or anything that sparks discussion and engagement.

The Currency of Conversation taps into the goal of creating messages that are highly regarded, discussed, and shared. I break these into three components or principles:

- **Relevance**: A message has currency when it has relevance.
- **Regard**: A message has relevance when the source from which it is shared is highly regarded.
- **Resonance**: A message gains recognition and high regard when it resonates.

You can apply this as an evaluation test for any message that you want to become shareable.

The First Female Leader

To conclude the Guyana 1992 election story, Dr. Jagan's party won convincingly, and he stayed in power until he died in 1997. His Chicago-born wife, Janet Rosenberg Jagan, was persuaded to run as president to carry on her husband's legacy (her opponent was Desmond Hoyte), and I handled her successful campaign. She thus became not only Guyana's first female president but also the first US-born woman to become president, albeit of a small South American republic.

Following a heart attack two years into her presidency, she decided to hand over the reins of power to the charismatic Bharrat

Jagdeo[14] (whose election campaigns I also successfully conducted), making him—at thirty-five years old—then one of the youngest heads of state in the world. It's worth noting that Bharrat Jagdeo, to his credit, signed legislation during his presidency that created a two-term limit for the office he held.

Through these historic political successes, I learned that creating *movements* rather than just election campaigns made the difference in how the populace responded and became engaged. Movements are built upon emotional structures and identifiable, relatable values more than they are on only policies and manifestos.

I saw these movements as a way to have a positive impact in my birthplace, Guyana. Then, in 2010, in my new home of Trinidad and Tobago, Kamla Persad-Bissessar[15] reached out to me to support her unlikely bid to become that island nation's first female prime minister. I jumped at the opportunity.

I had admired her for many years, beginning when she was a minister of education in the administration of former Prime Minister Basdeo Panday. I had told her then that if she ever decided to become prime minister to let me know.

The call came unexpectedly some eleven years later. It was the second time I had identified such potential. I had whispered the same thing to Bharrat Jagdeo when he was a junior minister of finance in Guyana. It would take some seven years before my vision for him became a reality. I began to believe I had an uncanny intuition for this, as I had identified others elsewhere with similar potential, but in those instances, I had not reached out. Reflecting upon it, I think

---

14 To read more about Bharrat Jagdeo sensational story, visit https://wsds.teriin.org/2012/assets/cv/bharrat_jagdeo_guyana.pdf

15 Dive deeper into Prime Minister Kamla Persad-Bissessar's compelling history at https://currentaffairs.adda247.com/kamla-persad-bissessars-historic-return-as-prime-minister-of-trinidad-and-tobago/amp/

it was my ability to observe how these candidates had a natural ability to connect with people on several levels, sometimes without even realizing it.

"I remember that you once told me, if I ever wanted to become prime minister, I should call you," Kamla Persad-Bissessar told me on that first call.

I replied that I would be honored to help her.

"I have no money," she explained matter-of-factly.

I took up the challenge of creating a powerful, resonant introduction to her campaign, despite the early absence of funding.

With high unemployment and a sitting prime minister who was considered to be aloof and arrogant, I looked for a place where I could position an inexpensive political message that would reflect the sentiment on the ground.

It came in the form of a small vacancy ad in the employment section of all of the local daily newspapers. That ad read simply:

Vacancy

Prime Minister

The ad went on to describe the qualifications of the candidate for the position of prime minister. Among the qualities sought were the specifications that the candidate for the post could not be arrogant or corrupt.

The ad was signed simply, "voiceofthepeople."

The earned media from this small vacancy ad was astounding. It was featured on the TV evening newscasts and picked up by several radio stations. It became a talking point across the islands and represented the first salvo of a political movement "of the people" later encapsulated in the sentence, "We will rise."

Kamla's rise to power also rode the wave of popularity through her own charisma, woven by carefully crafted messages that articulated precisely how the populace felt. She literally became the voice of the people.

While this is a story of a single successful campaign in an island nation, it represents the Currency of Conversation principle. The message of the campaign was shareable because it was relevant. The content resonated. The platform and community through which the message was shared were trustworthy and highly regarded.

Kamlamania, as it was called, took the island by storm and saw the election of Trinidad and Tobago's first female prime minister by a landslide. One of the key strategies we followed was a commitment to not run any attacks on the opposing party—the People's National Movement (PNM)—but instead to focus on the two individuals seeking the post of prime minister: Kamla Persad-Bissessar against the leader of the PNM and current prime minister, Patrick Manning.

The reason for this was my belief that he was the unpopular leader of a strong political organization, while she was the populist leader of a weaker political party. By focusing on the battle between these two individuals rather than the parties they led, I felt that we could score a victory.

There was a key Intangience principle at work here. We needed to *reframe the challenge.*

Our goal was no longer to win an election but to create a movement for change. We positioned Kamla as an almost matriarchal persona guiding a coalition labeled "The People's Partnership."

You can see the power of the Intangience methodology and the principles leading to logical, high-impact actions:

- Redefine political identities.
- Reframe the problem.
- Ignite a passionate following.
- Create resonant messaging.
- Reflect shared, intangible values through emotionally compelling stories.

I recall what happened the very moment the nation's first female prime minister was sworn in. She was expected to attend the usual formal celebratory gatherings, but a community in the south of the island had been stricken by severe flooding. When the swearing-in ceremony ended, the new prime minister skipped the galas and instead immediately got to work, traveling south and tending to the people who needed her there.

It was a defining moment for her. Headlines in every paper and on all electronic media shouted the story of her defiance of the usual celebration protocol to attend instead to "the people's business." Her campaign theme had been "We will rise!" and the prime minister's actions demonstrated her willingness to manifest the intangible value inherent in this message—to make it credible and authentic.

I chose to retire from political work years ago. I grew weary of the relentless, baseless, and libelous attacks aimed solely at discouraging me from excelling in the publicity work I carried out in the political arena. I gained the reputation as being the one to turn to, to create winning elections for the underdog or to create innovative campaigns for brands, with impressive results from a body of work that won some five hundred ADDY Awards. I grew to understand that I had developed a methodology that could shift perspectives and create a resonant message, allowing me to replicate this Science of Human Connection over and over again.

So, while I still work on brands that excite me through my innovation agency, my passion shifted from being challenged and excited by creating these successes in advertising and branding to showing, step by step, how these same principles can also be applied to living a more meaningful and fulfilled life.

But before I talk about that, there are a few more unusual stories that illustrate how effective the Intangience methodology is in creating engagement and conviction of opinion. One bizarre example of this is how a border intrusion and dispute saved a brewery from closure.

Intangience Insights

The Currency of Conversation depends on three points of reference that determine how the currency of a message, a brand's reputation, or its popularity is traded.

To inspire people to talk about and share a message, the story behind that message must be relevant, it must originate from a highly regarded source or community, and it must resonate at a deeply, fundamentally important level.

In the political sphere, a candidate's message must connect with those who are receiving it in this deep way, tapping into intangible values and communicating something important and aspirational about the character of the candidate and what they represent in the interest of the voters.

But these insights are not limited to the world of politics or brand building. This same Currency of Conversation and Connection can be used to launch a movement, transform a community, or spark awareness of a cause. Spend this currency wisely.

Intangience Inquiries

1. What are the three underlying principles that make a message more likely to be shared?
2. What was it about the candle ad that helped it resonate across all boundaries in Guyana?
3. Why couldn't most people recall Hillary Clinton's campaign slogan despite her outspending her rival Donald Trump?
4. Why did a simple vacancy ad in the employment section of the newspaper to fill the position of prime minister go so viral?

INTANGIENCE
INTANGIENCE
INTANGIENCE
INTANGIENCE
INTANGIENCE
INTANGIENCE
INTANGIENCE
INTANGIENCE
INTANGIENCE
INTANGIENCE
INTANGIENCE

CHAPTER FOUR

HOW A BORDER DISPUTE BECAME A BEER WAR

Perception is reality.

—LEE ATWATER

I define the emotional space that marketers seek to identify in brand development as *the geography of the mind.* In that landscape, an extraordinary and unique collection of experiences, beliefs, core identities, fears, and longings all coexist in each of us.

We live in these illusionary worlds, interpreting "reality" while sifting everything around us through our jaundiced interpretations.

Understanding this—and knowing how to use it—can save a business from shutting down or having to redefine its borders.

The chairman of Banks Brewery in Guyana came to me with a unique problem. Illegal imports of Polar Beer, a Venezuelan pilsner, were being transported across the long, porous border between Guyana and Venezuela and were flooding the local market, underselling Banks, the Guyanese brew.

The local brewery had protested vehemently to the government, but policing the huge border wasn't that easy. Banks Brewery had tried everything—bar promotions, price cuts, campaigns persuading Guyanese to buy local and enjoy the fresh brew—but nothing worked.

Amazingly, the iconic Banks Beer[16] was being swapped out for the cheaper import, Polar Beer. The situation had grown so bad that the brewery's production line was no longer operating every day, as the market demand had diminished so significantly. Were this situation to persist, it would mean that hundreds of employees would have to be let go.

You might assume that the brand loyalty for the local brew, built up over generations, would have been able to withstand any foreign import. There is, however, an inherent danger in believing that simply occupying a physical space translates automatically into brand strength. How you occupy the *emotional* space is far more important.

The quickness with which Guyanese traded out their go-to brand surprised me. It pointed to the absence of consumer affection and passion.

What did Banks Beer really *mean* to Guyanese?

What we learned was that the beer offered a taste they enjoyed at a price they could afford. That's pretty fragile ground on which to position your brand, as evidenced by the Polar Beer intrusion.

This wasn't simply a price problem, nor was it a taste preference. Those were simply illusions.

In fact, it was a brand identity crisis.

---

16 Visit https://www.bankssbeer.co.uk/ to learn more about Banks Beer.

We began by applying the Intangience Pillars of Purpose introspective process to reframe the problem and identify the solution. Let's take a look again in greater detail at this Intangience school of thought. The Pillars of Purpose involve the posing of three questions. They are perhaps the most important questions you can pose about your life and indeed for a brand. The three questions are the following:

Who am I? Try to see the brand identity from the consumer's perspective. Who are you to them? Think about your brand's core values and how they align with those of your consumers. Probe what the brand means to others beyond its functionality. What shared, intangible value does the brand embody that would resonate at a deeply fundamental level with consumers? Note the personification of the brand. Who am I? Not, what is it?

What is my purpose? Again, beyond the utilitarian purpose of the brand, what greater purpose does it serve consumers in a way that is important and essential to their lives? Explore the reason behind why the brand exists through the lens of intangible values.

The personification of the brand again is held. What is my purpose? Not, what is its purpose?

How will I be remembered? A crucial step in building brand architecture is to contemplate what lasting memory the brand will have for the consumer at various touchpoints, from packaging to promotions to all forms of publicity. What lingers with the consumer long after any form of encounter with the brand? What endures? What lives on to make it iconic and heartfelt? The question nudges you to contemplate what unforgettable and remarkable experiences the consumer will have with the brand. Once more, observe that the brand is personified: How will I be remembered? Not, how will it be remembered?

These three questions are like signposts that guide you to the Intangience insight—the emergence of a profound insight and universal truth, an intangible value and principle that is the true north of the brand message. It is what lies at the core of what needs to be understood about the context within which the brand exists. This insight defines the strategic direction of the business of the brand and even redefines the brand industry through what I call the industry of human relationship. (You will read more about this later in the book.)

Now let's see how the process was applied to the Banks Brewery challenge, where Polar Beer was being illegally imported into the country, flooding the market with a cheaper brew and a quality that Guyanese people seemed to enjoy and threatening the long-held dominance of the local brew.

HOW THE INTANGIECE PILLARS OF PURPOSE WERE APPLIED TO THE BANKS VS. POLAR BEER CHALLENGE

- Who am I?

I am the pride of Guyana.

- What is my purpose?

To create a deep sense of belonging.

- How will I be remembered?

As a celebration of who we are.

- What is the Intangience insight?

Everyone wants to have a sense of belonging.

Notice how the product was personified through the question-and-answer process, and recognize how the emotional space was explored. The Intangience insight presented the greatest challenge in this process. It was the pursuit of the big idea—one that connected the dots from the three probing questions to find that large perspective of what would guide how the creative strategy and execution were developed.

The brand emerged as the personification of everything it meant to be Guyanese. This wasn't about buying local. It was about Banks being the embodiment of national pride.

Once we identified that, the question of how to regain the market share stolen by Polar Beer was transformed into the challenge of how to evoke a sense of nationalism with the Banks brand.

The Colors of Patriotism

Think of a national flag. It is no more than a piece of fabric with a pattern of colors. But to those who identify with it as a citizen, it becomes a symbol of intense pride and a sense of belonging with deep emotions tied to it.

It is a powerful example of intangible values, demonstrating how meaning and emotional connection are derived.

Flags are flown on battleships, hoisted at sporting events to declare victories, and even planted on the moon. We have been conditioned to cry and die for all that a flag represents. A pattern of red, white, and blue might mean one thing in one place but not in a country whose national flag contains different color patterns.

I recall doing an ad to celebrate Independence Day in a country that was experiencing ethnic and political divisiveness on several levels. That ad featured a group of people with visual impairments running their hands over the country's national flag while calling out the colors and saying how much the flag meant to them. The ad ends with them standing outside the Offices of the Visually Impaired, wearing shirts that read, "Try to see the good in everyone."

It was a unique platform to have a group of people who were blind possess the ability to "see" that the only colors that should truly matter in the ethnically diverse country were those that defined them as citizens. The ad's message was that *seeing* represented an opportunity to focus on what was good, what unified people, not what divided or separated them.

The Guyana brewery situation offered a similar opportunity. I searched for the greatest point of unification around the flag and any other resonant point of Guyanese identity. Ironically, I found it right on the disputed border where the Venezuelan Polar Beer was intruding into Guyana.

The border dispute dates back nearly two hundred years, after a survey commissioned by the British government (Guyana was then British territory) set the border with Venezuela thirty thousand square miles further west than Venezuela felt was valid. Venezuela protested, claiming that the border should be set at the Essequibo River, effectively claiming two-thirds of what was then British Guiana.[17]

There is a song that is well known and loved in Guyana that chronicles the Guyanese perspective on the dispute. The song, composed by one of the country's iconic composers, Dave Martins, is called "Not a Blade of Grass." Its lyrics proudly declare, "We ain't giving up no mountain, we ain't giving up no tree, we ain't giving up no river, that belongs to we. Not one blue saki [a local bird], not one rice grain, not one kuras [a local fish], not a blade of grass."[18]

The Polar Beer incursion from Venezuela provided the perfect backdrop to ignite feelings about Guyana's patrimony. I proposed that we repurpose the song, adjusting the lyrics in part to, "We not giving up no river, we not giving up no tree, we not giving up the brewery that belongs to we."

The campaign grew into a celebration of everything it meant to be Guyanese: proud and patriotic, an embodiment of Banks Beer. The success was phenomenal. Within three months, there wasn't a Polar Beer to be seen in any bar anywhere in the country. Guyanese

---

17 "Venezuela Boundary Dispute, 1895–1899," Office of the Historian, United States Department of State, https://www.history.state.gov/milestones/1866-1898/venezuela.

18 Iknow, "Not a Blade of Grass Guyana Lyrics: Preserving Cultural Heritage," iKnow Guyana, June 18, 2023, https://iknowguyana.com/not-a-blade-of-grass-guyana-lyrics/.

from every walk of life rallied around the brand and even encouraged anyone seen consuming Polar Beer to stop.

So, what was the difference between the previous attempts by Banks Brewery and what I did? They focused on functionality, price points, and trying to persuade consumers to buy local. I reframed the challenge, focusing not on regaining market share but instead defining what the brew *meant* to Guyanese. It wasn't just a beer manufactured locally; it was what *being Guyanese* was proudly all about.

Once we identified that as the objective, the search for ways to achieve it became more evident. If Banks Beer was the brew that embodied Guyana's sense of self, then what was Polar Beer but a Venezuelan beer making incursions across "our" borders? The shift of perspective redrew the geography of the mind to reclaim the space of Guyana's true beer, as defined by the emotional connection laid bare by the border dispute created by the very origins of Polar Beer itself: Venezuela.

Forging a Caribbean Identity

Let me share an equally poignant example of how another beer brand redefined an entire region in a way that no previous attempts by political groupings had.

In this case, CARIB Brewery[19] on the island nation of Trinidad and Tobago hired me to promote its brew, Carib, as "The Beer of the Caribbean." This immediately presented a challenge. The Caribbean is made up of more than seven thousand islands, reefs, and cays, which are organized into thirty territories, including sovereign states, overseas departments, and dependencies. Many of these territories speak English, French, Spanish, or a local Creole dialect.

19 Visit https://caribbrewery.com/ to learn more about CARIB Brewery.

Each of these territories has its own national identity. No one from that part of the world identifies firstly with "the Caribbean." They are Antiguan or Jamaican or Trinidadian or an identity linked to one of those individual island nations. The only time someone who originates from this region says they are "from the Caribbean" is when they are explaining to a foreigner who, in their opinion, might be geographically limited and ignorant about the name of their specific island, so they surrender to the description.

The political and economic grouping referred to as the Caribbean Community, or CARICOM, has been attempting unsuccessfully to forge a collective identity for decades. The only success in this has been in the sport of cricket, where a "West Indies" team is chosen from ten island nations (all former colonies of the United Kingdom). But even that isn't truly representative of the entire Caribbean. So, there was no way Carib could achieve its lofty objective of being seen as a Caribbean beer by a population that didn't truly identify as a Caribbean people.

There was an even further challenge: The individual islands have their own distinctive brews, each with its own national identity. As an example, Red Stripe beer is Jamaican, Piton is the brew of Saint Lucia, Kubuli is from Dominica, and so on. The citizens of those countries are fiercely proud of their island brews.

The objective of linking Carib to the identity of *the* beer of the Caribbean was thus a very tall order.

The solution, once again, was developed through the Intangience approach.

Pillars of Purpose: The Carib Brew Caribbean Identity

- Who am I?

I am what defines one of the most picturesque places on the planet.

- What is my purpose?

To show the world who we are.

- How will I be remembered?

As an expression of my Caribbean island pride and excitement.

- Intangience insight

Everyone wants to be acknowledged for who they truly are.

What emerged from these insights was a campaign that grew to be the most successful ever run by CARIB Brewery, garnering over twenty-four million views and an outpouring of positive responses across the region and elsewhere.

Themed "Can you feel it?" the campaign captured the essence of the Caribbean as perhaps never seen before in terms of the varied cultural expressions laid out by extremely high production values and the use of iconic music personalities, such as DJ Khaled, who introduces an escape to this idyllic region as a just reward for the hard work of business people assembled in a boardroom during the pandemic.[20]

Intangience Insights

Why did more than thirty Caribbean island nations rally around this production and so strongly identify with it? What brought this disparate region together to identify with the singularity of the

20 "CARIB Brewery: DJ KHALED SAYS: CAN YOU FEEL IT?," n.d., https://caribbrewery.com/dj-khaled-says-can-you-feel-it/.

Caribbean as a shared identity? The answer lies in the application of the techniques and devices that are identified in the Intangience methodology as the Science of Human Connection. Coke is the best example of how these techniques and devices are developed and deployed. That brand's defined ambition is to get you to "enjoy the brand even when you're not consuming it."

Coke masters the game—from printing people's names on its label to forge personal identities, to offering free Coke through vending machines at college campuses that can only be enjoyed when two bottles are brought together to open the beverage, and even to creating the world's first drinkable ad, which features people pulling from an interactive "straw." These are all examples of techniques that reinforce the brand's desire to embody human connection.

For the Carib beer campaign, we used the simple device of a flag to allow the Caribbean audience to have that sense of emotional connection and identity with a brand that was seeking to override the strong individuality of each island. By creating a platform for the Caribbean music and culture as never seen before, we made each island proud to be a part of the collective identity. They felt individually acknowledged and celebrated by the world. True to the campaign theme "Can you feel it?" they did!

This was achieved by featuring the various island nation flags waved by models at various points in the video and as a signature at the end. By allowing individual Caribbean national identities to coexist, from Jamaica in the north to Guyana in the south, we were able to create an ad campaign that celebrated the common cultural heritage and to have the Carib brand embody the intangible value of bringing everyone together in celebration of who they are. There was no obvious display of the Carib brew. It appeared as organic as sand on the beach. There was not even any mention of the brand name lyrically in the music video. This all helped it to resonate and override the market resistance to beers that were not national.

These are clear examples of how intangible values connect us all. The intangible matters much more than mere functionality. It was the national identity of the Guyanese that saved Banks Brewery—not the product itself but what it was creatively shown to embody. It was the flags of the Caribbean woven into a strong music video that created a collective identity that didn't exist before—one that could become the embodiment of the Carib brew that exemplified the Caribbean.

The intangible matters much more than mere functionality.

To understand the power of the intangible is to know what matters most in human connection.

As was referenced earlier in chapter three, water is an example of a product that is available in most countries for free, yet consumers are willing to buy.

Many brands of bottled water vie for a share of a global market estimated at over $300 billion. It boggles the mind when one considers the fact that the main competitor of the bottled water is from the tap. In fact, many major bottled water brands are foisting tap water on consumers and selling it for five-hundred times the price! Research has shown that, apart from the fact that consumers cannot distinguish the difference in taste between one and another, there is in fact no difference between the water from the tap and those of many of the bottled brands. *In some cases, the quality of tap water was actually purer than those of bottled water!* So, what would cause consumers to pay as much as $85 for a champagne-like packaged bottle of water—or any form of bottled water for that matter? And the answer lies in part, yes, by the sense of assurance they have that it is purer; but deeper than that it is by buying into the intangible values inherent in these brands.

In Youngme Moon's brilliant book *Different*, she references the absurd lengths to which some of these well known water brands go in trying to differentiate themselves from each other and sell their "purity." She quotes from marketing material of the super premium brand of water, Voss:

> "Voss Artesian Water comes from an aquifer in the pristine nature of Southern Norway, protected from pollutants by layers of rock and sand, producing a pure water unlike any other.When tapped into, the aquifer is pressurized enough to allow the water to rise up naturally through the ground without the use of mechanical pumps. Because the water is protected by this impermeable layer, it does not come into contact with the air or other pollutants."[21]

Not to be undone by Voss this is how the FIJI brand of water describes its own purity.

> "Preserved and protected by its source and location, FIJI Water's aquifer is in a virgin ecosystem at the edge of a primitive rainforest, a continent away from the nearest industrialized civilization. Our rainfall is purified by equatorial winds after traveling thousands of miles across the Pacific Ocean. Winds that carry acid rain and pollutants to other parts of the planet just do not come our way. So if you ever wondered what really pure water tastes like, just open a bottle of FIJI Water."[22]

21 Moon, *Different*, 64.

22 Moon, *Different*, 75.

I will now demonstrate in an exercise—one that usually takes me about sixty seconds—how the Intangience methodology will create an authentic connection with a made up brand of water with no distinction in packaging, price, nor purity.

Consider our offering to be a simple, plain, purified bottle of water.

Here you will see how utilitarian purpose isn't attempted but, rather, an intangible value embodied in the brand becomes a compelling piece of persuasion. First, let us apply the Pillars of Purpose process to our bottled water.

- Who am I?

I am the relief you seek.

- What is my purpose?

To bring rejuvenation to a thirsty world.

- How will I be remembered?

As a refreshing source of kindness.

- What is the Intangience insight?[23]

No one in the world should ever go thirsty.

Note how powerful the insight is, developed through the introspective Pillars of Purpose process. All of a sudden, an emotional connection based upon a universally agreeable intangible value emerges and becomes an embodiment of our water brand.

---

23 This explores what we call the industry of human relationships within which the particular product operates. It's more than just the sector of manufacturing your product is operating in. That's all just functional. The industry of human relationships is defined by the shared intangible values embodied in the brand that the consumer strongly identifies with and deems hugely important. Coke, as an example, isn't just in the beverage sector—it is in the human connection industry.

Imagine if the phrase "*Because no one in the world should ever go thirsty*" were plastered on every billboard of our water brand, on all social media posts, on our packaging, trucks transporting the product, emblazoned on the uniforms of employees. Imagine on very hot days, our water trucks are seen giving out free bottles of our brand of water to the homeless, construction workers, and even to schoolchildren. These acts of compassion and genuine concern become our social media story and one we implore others to enjoin as we look to fulfill our mission in ensuring *no one in the world ever goes thirsty*.

All advertising features emotionally compelling stories of our brand of water being freely distributed when needed in the most thirst quenching moments, manifesting our brand purpose. When you go to a supermarket or any distribution point, how much resonance and recognition would our brand of water hold?

An authentic brand differentiation would have been created without any attempt at making outlandish claims of how pure our water extraction processes were or investing in fanciful packaging. The appeal would just have been created through identifying a powerful shared intangible value that resonated deeply with consumers.

That's the power of shared intangible values and the science of human connection.

Intangience Inquiries

1. Why is it important for a brand to occupy emotional space?
2. Why do flags hold such significance for us?
3. Why does emotionality mean more than functionality in a product offering?
4. What does mapping the geography of the mind when trying to reach a consumer mean?

CHAPTER FIVE

HOW FREEDOM OF THE PRESS WAS TRANSFORMED INTO FREEDOM *FROM* THE PRESS

If liberty means anything at all, it means the right to tell people what they do not want to hear.

—GEORGE ORWELL[24]

Imagine a frail old Indian man, an environmentalist, sitting for more than ninety days on a sidewalk outside the offices of a prime minister. He claims to be engaged in a hunger strike to protest the construction of a highway.

The incredible thing about this is not the fact that the hunger strike had been going on for ninety days, but that this protester had sworn off both food and water! That he could still find the strength and energy to continue this dusk-to-dawn vigil for more than ninety days should have defied any mortal's physical capacity. Yet the media coverage ignored the realities of biology, choosing instead to focus on the old man's cause and his personal sacrifice and to elevate him to heroic levels.

24 George Orwell, "The Freedom of the Press" (written 1944), *Times Literary Supplement*, September 15, 1972.

At the time, I was assisting the government of Trinidad and Tobago with imaging and public relations. I received a call from the prime minister.

She expressed her concern for the environmentalist's presumed failing health and was worried about how the community would be impacted if he were to die. I assured her that this was unlikely since, if the elderly environmentalist sitting on the pavement outside her office was genuinely on a hunger strike that included depriving himself of water, he would have perished a long time ago. She replied that while this was obvious, he could still perish in a weakened state. I promised her that I would create a platform to question the legitimacy of the protestor's claims.

I pressed a few reporters to question the environmentalist on how he could survive without the need for hydration, much less food, for such a long period. His answer was not only astounding but again went largely unquestioned by the media and others.

He told the reporters that he would get up very early in the morning and go into his garden, where the dew was forming upon the trees and plants. While there, he would quietly meditate and absorb the moisture that hung in the air!

That he found a way to survive without water through some form of osmosis made him a unique human species indeed.

Perhaps conscious of the fact that some people were beginning to question how his hunger strike could go on so long, the protesting environmentalist reportedly collapsed on the pavement. He was rushed to a nearby hospital, where his vitals were checked.

The alleged results were as expected: no dehydration. All of his vital organs were functioning perfectly. For all intents and purposes, he was in good shape for just about anyone, much less someone who claimed to have not eaten or so much as sipped a drop of water for more than ninety days!

Frustrated by the absence of public discussion about this farce and irritated by the praise he continued to receive for his charade, I developed a series of ads that mimicked a *National Geographic* documentary, in which an unusual creature was discovered on the pavement outside the prime minister's office. This species, the ad explained, was unique in its ability to endure months of food and water deprivation.

It was a comic parody of what was taking place daily. In response, the ads were banned by the media, but not because of a legal challenge—in fact, the attorneys for the media houses had cleared the material. It was the editors who objected to the ads, stating that they were, in their opinion, "in poor taste." As a further backdrop to this, the ads placed by the environmentalist group represented by the protestor in the same media contained several falsehoods but were allowed.

I was furious and unwilling to allow this suffocation of public discourse to persist.

I reached out to an attorney from the United States and another from Canada to argue the case for free media modeled after the then relevant standards in both those countries.

I also created a campaign with its own website called bannedbythemedia.com. We created some dynamic ads. One featured a man passionately speaking about his right to be heard until a hand emerges from behind and clasps his mouth. These black-and-white videos appeared everywhere on social media, and, within a week, we had more than seven hundred thousand views.

I also created my own for-hire protest group to mirror the antics of the hunger striker. Hundreds of protestors were bused into the city, wearing "Banned by the Media" T-shirts, their mouths taped by the image of a closed zipper. They took to the streets, handing out flyers while the song "Turn Down for What" blared loudly.

While we attracted a lot of attention and even stormed the newsrooms of the media houses, none of them covered the activity. They decided our Banned by the Media campaign should itself be banned by the media.

Ironically, this worked in our favor. Public interest was piqued. What was this material that the media didn't want them to see? Who gave these editors the right to determine what was in poor taste when their very attorneys had cleared the ads to run?

Interest in our campaign and cause grew to the extent that one media house folded under the pressure and began to cover the issue. I was beginning to achieve my purpose. Questions about the protestor's ninety days without water and food grew, and the veil of his victimhood began to fall. The decision by one media network to run our material seemed to create a dent in the unified position of the Trinidad & Tobago Publishers & Broadcasters Association, which invited me to a conciliatory meeting.

It was a tense discussion. They clearly stated their right to refuse material that, in their opinion, was offensive in any way. I countered by saying that we also had a right to hold them to account and that this kind of censorship could not be in the interest of a democratic society in which all views and opinions need to be heard and debated. They claimed that my ads were demeaning. I countered by pointing out the deception of the hunger striker, whose desire for popularity and heroism was matched only by the media's willingness to leave him unchallenged. I expressed my anger that I had been forced into doing their job, pointing out the naked reality of this "Emperor of the Environment."

To be clear, I didn't object to the environmentalist's right to protest. In fact, I admired his courage of conviction. I had no objection to his staging a hunger strike in which he denied himself food and water but to pretentiously twist what seemed to be a false narrative upon an unsuspecting public and a compliant media was too much to bear. The absurd street theater he staged each day on the pavement called into question, in my view, his credibility on some of the very claims he was perhaps legitimately making on the construction of the highway and its damaging effects on the environment. If he could lie about his hunger strike, then he was, in turn, compromising the legitimacy of his claims.

Amplifying the Message

The Intangience principle in play here comes from the school of thought referenced as the Science of Human Connection: the techniques and devices developed and deployed to amplify and clarify your message. In this case, it was the arrival of a *National Geographic* team to conduct research on this rather unique, humanlike creature with the ability to survive without water (never mind food) by absorbing moisture through his pores.

The "hunger strike" would go on for an astounding nine months before the environmentalist decided to call off his charade. By the end, he had modified his claim, explaining that he had been surviving on tulsi leaves (an herb used in Ayurvedic and Hindu practices), water, coconut water, and an occasional cup of dhal.[25] He began to refer to his act as a "fast" rather than a hunger strike, saying that although he felt weak, his fasting had not seriously affected his health.

25 "Wayne Surviving on Tulsi Leaves, Water . . . Day 189," *Daily Express*, March 22, 2015, https://www.trinidadexpress.com/news/local/wayne-surviving-on-tulsi-leaves-water/article_15384af6-2503-5e02-8fbf-57c354c63e22.html.

You might recall that, earlier in this book, I explained that while I might convince you of a fact, it wouldn't change the way you feel and so would not compel you to shift your position or opinion. This campaign was a case in point. It should have been obvious to everyone that this protestor was indulging in absurdism. But he inspired a lot of people to identify with his cause, and the support went beyond whether or not he was actually shunning food and water or was close to death.

In fact, I received a call from a dear colleague of mine in the advertising fraternity, the head of another agency, who expressed dismay and disappointment at my attempts to discredit what she described as a "hero of the country." She said that even her very young son was concerned for him. I asked her if she believed that this man was genuinely on a hunger strike, to which she replied that he looked very frail. I pointed out that he was by nature a very thin and small-framed individual, but that it would have been impossible for anyone to be deprived of food and water for so long. She replied that I was missing the point.

Trying to get her to understand the medical reality of his claim was impossible. She was emotionally invested in the elderly environmentalist and what he represented to her. The false reports of his near-death condition were lost on her. She had surrendered her independent thought about this to the emotional tug of his pavement protest and the myth of his slow and steady decline.

When such deception takes over common sense, you have to use the same kind of dramatic techniques and devices to convey your message at an equally emotional level.

For those who ask how Donald Trump survived his own words and actions, the mainstream media, the January 6 incitement of insurrection, the courts, and a battery of criminal charges, the answer lies in how he used each of those situations to his advantage through political theatrics, along with techniques and devices for connecting with people at an emotional level.

Once again, it's the Science of Human Connection. In this case, it's the three principles of persuasion:

- Identifying the purpose that best serves the audience
- Igniting a passionate following
- Tuning into current behaviors, opinions, trends, and the overall emotional landscape, or what I call a *polyphonic understanding* of what is taking place

Trump didn't just stoke the fears of unbridled immigration; he pounced on opportunities to dramatize it by antics such as referencing an absurd post—later refuted by the very person who posted it—that immigrants from Haiti were eating "the cats and dogs, the pets" in Springfield, Ohio.[26]

The absurdity of his statement did more than simply draw attention to the immigration challenges being faced in that community. It sparked fiery discussion about the situation.

This is a strategy Trump uses over and over to capture attention. Psychologists will tell you that there is a correlation between attention and memory, so the technique of drawing someone's attention using dramatic methods will also reinforce their recall. If you did not recall before that there were twenty-five thousand Haitian immigrants in Springfield,[27] Donald Trump's outrageous and outlandish claim that

26 Merlyn Thomas and Mike Wendling, "Donald Trump Repeats Baseless Claim About Haitian Immigrants Eating Cats and Dogs in Springfield, Ohio," September 15, 2024, https://www.bbc.com/news/articles/c77l28myezko.

27 Mandy Gambrell, "Haitian Immigrants in Springfield, Ohio: Why They Chose This City," *Dayton Daily News*, September 12, 2024, https://www.daytondailynews.com/local/haitian-immigrants-in-springfield-ohio-why-they-chose-this-city/2YSECZBYS5DYTF35SC5U4QS5SI/.

there were illegal Haitian immigrants consuming people's pets shifted your focus to this population.

Now, I'm not advocating that this is either a recommended tactic or a moral justification. Quite the opposite. I find it reprehensible. Did it work? Unfortunately, yes!

When Joe Biden made a gaffe about Trump supporters being garbage after a speaker at a 2024 Trump rally said that Puerto Rico was a "floating island of garbage," Donald Trump's reaction was to don a garbage collector's outfit and jump into the seat of a garbage truck with "Trump | Vance" emblazoned on it. When Kamala Harris spoke of her working early in life at a McDonald's, Trump arranged to be at a McDonald's, wearing its uniform and serving "customers" at its drive-thru!

Each of these incidents was carried on all media platforms, the images burning into our memories. Trump is a made-for-media political showman, demonstrating how to create dramatic impact in the most outlandish of ways. Who else could find himself convicted while producing merchandise such as mugs with his mug shot and gaining hundreds of millions of dollars in donations out of a sordid event?

For all the analysis of the things that went wrong for the Democratic Party in the 2024 US presidential election (and there were many), the simple truth is that Donald Trump was far more effective at communicating one memorable message after another while positioning his candidacy around the idea that he would "drain the swamp" and "demolish the deep state."

Message Resonance

Let's look at one more example from the 2024 US presidential election to understand the methodology for creating a message that resonates.

When basketball legend LeBron James endorsed Kamala Harris, it was considered a huge plug from an iconic sports personality with more than 159 million followers on Instagram alone. It was anticipated that this would resonate particularly powerfully with young Black male voters. It didn't seem to make a difference though, as Donald Trump gained more support among Black voters over his results four years earlier, including winning the votes of 24 percent of Black men.[28]

Here's how the LeBron message could have been better developed:

[LeBron's voice-over] *The scores are tied, and we're down to the final few seconds that will determine the future of America. Everything comes down to this point.*

[Shot of LeBron about to shoot a basketball]

[Image freezes]

[LeBron's voice] *But it's up to you this time. Make it count for America. Make it count for you and future generations.*

Score one with me for Kamala Harris.

[Buzzer sounds to rapturous applause]

The response to this would have been visceral. And it would have played to the very popularity in the game of basketball for which LeBron is legendary. I'm not professing that this would have made a difference, but it certainly would have created the impact by being emotive rather than just being another celebrity endorsement.

That's the Science of Human Connection: using techniques and devices that resonate. Such a message would have been shared millions of times by adoring fans and would have connected at a more emotional level.

---

28 "Interactive: How Key Groups of Americans Voted in 2024," *PBS News*, November 7, 2024, https://www.pbs.org/newshour/politics/interactive-how-key-groups-of-americans-voted-in-2024-according-to-ap-votecast.

Intangience Insights

You have to learn how to direct the attention of the audience.

I learned this lesson clearly when the owner of a new sports bar contacted me. He was struggling with the challenge of identifying how to successfully introduce his sports bar to the public. He complained bitterly that he had spent all of his money on building and equipping the sports bar, sparing no expense to make it the best it could be. He claimed that it would redefine expectations in the sports bar industry.

His request? He wanted me to make the sports bar's location memorable and the brand a talking point.

With only a very small media budget available, I decided on a piece of street theater. I hired about a dozen amateur actors to assemble in small groups for over half an hour and simply point up to the sky at a time of day when there was a lot of traffic.

Twelve people standing at a busy street corner looking up at the sky and pointing excitedly were certain to gather the attention of passersby. You would probably look up yourself to see what all the excitement was about.

But it didn't stop there. I had various people call radio and TV stations to ask what was happening at this street corner. Why, they asked, were so many people pointing up at the sky?

You have to learn how to direct the attention of the audience.

Within an hour, scores of other onlookers had joined my group of actors to witness what was not there. In fact, some people actually claimed to be seeing ... *something*, although what they thought they saw varied significantly.

There was wide media coverage of this nonevent. We eventually explained that this was nothing more than a publicity event and what our excitable group was actually pointing to was the building where the new sports bar would soon open. But still, there were photos of the spectacle in the press, and one television station actually reported on the incident on the evening newscast.

It was an example of how to literally direct attention and create a buzz about something that wasn't even there.

These scenarios reinforce how important it is to understand the need to entertain, engage, and entice an audience. We are all naturally curious creatures with an innate desire to figure things out.

As one of the principles of Intangience attests: You gain someone's attention best when you can hold their interest. Merely stating facts or selling benefits isn't enough. Creative techniques and devices are necessary to stimulate interest and make content shareable.

Intangience Inquiries

1. What was the creative device that made the false hunger strike of the environmentalist such a talking point, and why did it work?
2. Why did the political messaging of Trump gain so much media attention?
3. What are the three principles of the Science of Human Connection?
4. How do you best gain someone's attention?

INTANGIENC

INTANGIENC
INTANGIENC
INTANGIENC
INTANGIENC
INTANGIENC
INTANGIENC
INTANGIENC
INTANGIENC
INTANGIENC
INTANGIENC

CHAPTER SIX

HOW GANG LEADERS IN THE CARIBBEAN RESPONDED POSITIVELY TO A MESSAGE

The most dangerous creation of any society is the man who has nothing to lose.

—JAMES BALDWIN[29]

The toughest challenge of my career was when the Ministry of National Security on the island of Trinidad and Tobago invited me to develop a communication campaign that would address gang violence in a high-risk community.

The area called Beetham was so renowned as a haven for criminal activity and gang warfare that not even cops wanted to venture there.

The ask for a campaign to address the issue became the biggest test of my Intangience methodology. How could I connect with gang leaders in a way that they would even listen, much less respond positively? I certainly had no intention of developing a campaign in which it appeared that the government was merely paying lip service to the needs of an impoverished community overrun by criminals.

29 James Baldwin, *The Fire Next Time* (Random House, 1990).

I also resisted advice to launch a gun amnesty program or develop some similar initiative. Such efforts had been attempted before in other areas, and they had been unsuccessful. Neither did I want some vacuous appeal to gang leaders to "do the right thing" and give up a life of crime. I needed something that would demonstrate that even these hardened gangsters could be reached with a resonant message.

Many of the gang leaders were young men, most of whom would not live past their midtwenties at best. Some were merely teenagers, and the crimes they committed were often brutal.

For them, death was nothing to be feared. In fact, going out in a gun battle was often glorified as being heroic in a sense.

I recall watching a video of a car that crashed during a police pursuit. The occupants were surrounded by law enforcement officers with their guns trained on those inside. The police demanded that they exit the vehicle with their hands raised, and two did so—first one, followed by another. These two were immediately ordered to lie on the ground with their hands behind their backs. They were then handcuffed and taken away.

But still, the others remained in the vehicle. The tension built. There was clearly no escape for them. They had seen their colleagues arrested but at least unharmed. They knew that their only option, if they wanted to stay alive, was to do the same.

One by one, they exited the vehicle. But each came out firing at the police, and each was, in turn, cut down by returning gunfire. In the end, three young men lay dead on the roadside.

The video of this suicidal behavior was shared widely on social media. I believe that those who came out of the car while firing pointlessly at the fully armed cops encircling their crashed vehicle knew they would die, but they also knew that their final act of bravado would be recorded and seen as a proud legacy—proof of a life of defiance and unrattled courage.

Growing up in a community where they felt life offered virtually nothing, their own lives had become of little value. So, whether they took their own life or someone else took it was of no consequence, since everything else had already been taken from them.

The community in which they lived, Beetham, is located opposite a landfill called La Basse, where mounds of rubbish are often burned. This stretch of land, located on the cusp of the city entrance, emanates such a foul odor that it permeates your vehicle when you drive through it. Most people drive through this areas as quickly as possible, with their windows tightly closed.

The people who live in this area—the citizens of the Beetham community—are affected daily by those toxic fumes, but they don't have the option to roll up their windows and speed past. They have to numb themselves to the odor, just as they must numb themselves to so much else affecting them. It is not uncommon for the area to have feces flowing through the streets, even into homes, as a result of decaying sewage pipes that frequently burst and then remained unrepaired for extended periods of time.

There is only one highway that takes you into the city, and that highway runs along Beetham. This accident of geography gave the members of that community a tiny bit of power. They had some small measure of control over this critical traveling conduit, and every once in a while, they would let the government know it. They would storm the road, stoning vehicles and strewing debris from the landfill, obstructing the highway. It would take hours to clear and would create, at a minimum, a major inconvenience—if not fear and sometimes even injury to the traveling public.

The landfill located next to Beetham was the unofficial gathering place. The people who lived in Beetham went there often to rummage through garbage for just about anything they could eat or use or sell or repurpose in some way. As each garbage truck arrived, you could see people running beside it. Some would even jump on the back to ride ahead of the others in order to be first in line for the truck's off-loading.

It was a place of bleak possibilities. It was also a place where criminal activity was constant and growing.

This was the challenge I faced: to somehow find a way to connect with this community and create a message for the gang leaders that would resonate, that would be relevant, and that would inspire those who heard it. It was in the face of this challenge that I developed what I believe to this day to be one of the most significant successes of my long career.

The Risk of Losing Hope

The campaign commissioned by the Ministry of National Security offers a powerful case study for the Intangience methodology. Let me share the step-by-step framework I used, beginning, of course, with the three foundational questions:

Intangience: Pillars of Purpose **Client:** Ministry of National Security

Objective: To deliver a message of hope to gang leaders in a high-risk area.

Applying the introspective process of the Pillars of Purpose, three critical questions were posed to understand the gang leaders' perspective.

- Who am I?

I'm a strong leader in my community.

- What is my purpose?

To get respect, control, and money.

- How will I be remembered?

As one who defied every authority and was feared and respected by the gangster community.

The answers that emerged from these probes provided an understanding of the gang leaders' mindset, their perspective on life, and the role they felt destined to play.

These three questions guided us to a larger viewpoint from which a profound insight arrived.

It wasn't easy to pluck this deeper understanding of the task at hand, but when filtered through the three touchpoints from the questions, they became signposts that directed us to find a commonality of the human condition related to what we intended to share as a compelling, resonant message.

The Intangience insight:

Everyone needs someone to look up to in life.

Notice how the insight about that human condition emerged from the introspection on the gang leaders' perspective.

The strategy and communication campaign mapped by the Intangience methodology had an amazing impact.

Everyone needs someone to look up to in life.

The dramatic launch of the initiative unfolded in real time this way:

A convoy of luxury SUVs with dark, tinted windows wound its way slowly along the dusty roads leading into the Beetham community in the middle of the day.

Suddenly, they came to a halt. The engines hummed. For a minute or two, no one disembarked from the vehicles.

Slowly, a crowd of curious onlookers began to arrive. Some people came tentatively at first, testing the safety of this unfolding scene. Others peeped through the broken windows and doorways of the small shacks in which they lived. You could hear a murmur growing into a loud chatter as curiosity built.

Eventually, a man emerged from one of the SUVs. He was a huge, imposing figure, standing seven feet one and weighing 325 pounds.

Towering over everyone around him, he ambled toward a dilapidated basketball court right in the middle of Beetham, holding a basketball. He casually began throwing hoops.

Within minutes, the word spread throughout the community and around the island. Incredible as it seemed, unbelievable as it was to those who had gathered, Shaquille O'Neal[30]—the iconic, legendary basketball player—was there in Beetham, playing on its court!

Quickly, the media converged on the site. People tuned in from everywhere to what was taking place as the drama unfolded. Once the initial shock and disbelief faded within the Beetham community, the excitement became palpable.

Shaq was a truly heroic figure to everyone in the community, regardless of age, and he responded to their joy generously and charmingly. More significantly, as he spoke with the people there, he shared a powerful message about his own early years growing up in a community very much like Beetham.

---

30 Read more about NBA great Shaquille O'Neal at https://www.hoophall.com/hall-of-famers/shaquille-oneal/.

Images of him lifting young children up to the basketball hoop were etched forever in the hearts and minds of those gathered there and the hundreds of thousands who later saw them in the media.

But it wasn't just the arrival of Shaq in the community that made this campaign successful. He was there to launch an initiative I created called The Hoop of Life, a basketball competition open to gang members playing together on different teams for a coveted trophy, bragging rights, and 1.5 million Trinidad and Tobago dollars, which went back into the community for various projects.

The response from the gang members was overwhelming. So much so that the initiative was expanded to cover sixty communities and a total of 720 players.

For the entire duration of the competition, there was not a single act of violence at any of the well-attended games. Not on the court or in the crowds that enthusiastically attended.

The campaign won several ADDY Awards, helped in no small part by Anil Hardit-Singh, who both composed the outstanding soundtrack and directed the brilliant TV spot. But the achievement I'm proudest of is how this message resonated and the way in which the nuances of the ad's script were understood by the gang members when we asked them about it.

The Hoop of Life TV script:

I always knew the time would come ...
Some things are just inevitable.
I believe ...
the end that arrives
begins in the moment
we choose a certain path in life,
and wherever that journey takes us,
I believe ...

whatever we become,
goes right back down
to how we look up
to see ourselves in the future.
I believe ...
In myself.
I see the world spinning
out of control
only when we miss the point of it all.
I believe ...
things will only change when we do.
Those are the rules of the game in life.
So, let the courts decide.
Because the time will come, as it must,
when opportunity will arrive.
I believe ...
We will come full circle,
In the Hoop of Life,
To become somebody we've always looked up to,
when we believe.

Phrases such as "I believe the end arrives in the moment we choose a certain path in life" spoke to their vulnerable lives—lives that were typically cut down early and violently.

"Let the courts decide" alluded to both the basketball courts and the criminal courts with which these young men were so familiar.

Throughout the script, the carefully crafted language intentionally focused on emotional touchpoints designed to reflect the way these young men lived. The very game of basketball was one they identified with and was often their only means of escape from their tense and dangerous lifestyle.

For me, this entire initiative was the biggest test of Intangience and one of the most meaningful. It was proof that the methodology could be applied effectively to create a positive impact, even in the most challenging circumstances. It was to the credit of Prime Minister Kamla Persad Bissessar to have had both the foresight and courage to commit to an innovative initiative that created such an impact.

Intangience Insights

Meeting sales targets, shifting brand perceptions, and winning over voters were successes in their own right. But creating peace and harmony? That's another level of meaningful, purpose-driven, achievable goals.

All of the principles and schools of thought of Intangience were in play throughout the development of the Hoop of Life initiative. The introspective Pillars of Purpose exercise allowed us to see the landscape through the perspective of the gang leaders. The profound insight "everyone needs someone to look up to in life" guided our work, encapsulating the entire essence of what we needed to do to connect successfully with this tough, hardened group of young men who had hitherto seemed impossible to reach.

The Currency of Conversation, which addresses how to create a message that is shareable and popular, can clearly be seen in the way Hoop of Life was developed. It wasn't launched at a fancy event with government officials and business leaders in attendance. It happened without fanfare, without any big announcements or introductions. Maintaining that surprise and keeping what was going to happen quiet ahead of time was admittedly one of the tougher parts of the execution, but I insisted on it.

Shaq was flown by private jet to Trinidad. He was ushered quickly through a special entrance at the airport and whisked away in a convoy of vehicles to the prime minister's official residence. From there, he, along with the prime minister and a few other officials, was taken straight to the basketball court in Beetham.

The dramatic impact of this clandestine operation was integral to the outcome. It became a talking point, a highly shareable moment. Shaq's presence on their basketball court was a relevant message shared by the members of the Beetham community themselves.

Shaq was there, speaking directly to them. His story was theirs. They held him in high regard. His message resonated.

The other Intangience school of thought that was evident in the Hoop of Life was the Science of Human Connection, which explains the importance of the techniques and devices used to make communication work: igniting a passionate following, identifying a greater purpose, and having a polyphonic understanding of the environment in which the intended message is being conveyed.

Shaq ignited a passionate following around a game they played and loved. The greater purpose was served through the promise of the Hoop of Life prize: winning bragging rights *and* the money deployed to help their community. None of that would have been possible without our ability to read the play and tap into the pulse of the community and their lifestyle, attitudes, and behavior.

Note as well how the story wasn't about changing their lives or attempting to persuade them to leave a life of crime. It was an emotional experience of hope from someone they looked up to, someone who exemplified what they most wanted: a better life and to be respected.

The basketball competition launched by Shaq embodied all of that. It offered a path to something better.

That campaign remains, to this day, my most powerful example of how you can reach anyone once you see life from their perspective, understand what truly drives them, and authentically connect using the Intangience practices.

Remember, something only has value when it holds *meaning* for those who wish to possess it.

Intangience Inquiries

1. How did the Pillars of Purpose introspective purpose achieve a better understanding of the gangsters' minds, and what was the significance of the insight "everyone needs someone to look up to in life"?
2. What would have been the difference if Shaq had been introduced at a formal function, perhaps at a hotel or other environment, by the government?
3. Can you identify the three principles of the Currency of Conversation in the Hoop of Life campaign?

INTANGIENCE
INTANGIENCE
INTANGIENCE
INTANGIENCE
INTANGIENCE
INTANGIENCE
INTANGIENCE
INTANGIENCE
INTANGIENCE
INTANGIENCE
INTANGIENCE
INTANGIENCE

CHAPTER SEVEN

HOW TO DEVELOP A SIXTH SENSE OF INVISABILITY

I am not afraid of storms, for I am learning how to sail my ship.

—LOUISA MAY ALCOTT[31]

If we could reframe every challenge in our lives in a way that best guides us to a solution, how much happier we would be and what a better world it might become.

I love to quote and follow Einstein's theory that "the formulation of a problem is often more essential than its solution."[32] It simply means that if you frame a problem incorrectly, you may arrive at the wrong answer or solution.

As an example, in my country, Guyana, where there is often ethnic tension because of its past, do we ask how to create harmony and promote understanding among ethnic groups, or do we ask how to create social and economic equality? In this particular example,

31 Louisa May Alcott, *Little Women*, 150th anniversary edition (SeaWolf Press, 2019), 497.

32 Oleg Komlik, "Albert Einstein on the Power of Ideas and Imagination in Science," *Economic Sociology & Political Economy*, January 8, 2016, https://www.economicsociology.org/2016/01/08/albert-einstein-on-the-power-of-ideas-and-imagination-in-science/.

I'm not advocating which is better; I'm merely illustrating how the framing of a problem changes how we perceive both the challenge and the likelihood of discovering a different solution as a result.

This is one of the critical elements of Intangience. During the pandemic, some businesses thrived, while others just couldn't be sustained. Sometimes, this was because of an inability or reluctance to redefine the business or simply to allocate resources differently by reframing what the new challenges were. It's worth noting that, during the pandemic, our branding and advertising business grew simply because we became more innovative than ever and offered clients different approaches to deliver results amid the toughest of circumstances.

Here is one example of how we countered the lockdowns and bar restrictions for a beer brand.

The client had projected a 2.5 percent decline in their business because of the pandemic. There were multiple factors for this gloomy projection: closed bars, lockdowns, declining disposable income, job losses, and a generally poor outlook for just about every business. Carnival celebrations—a season perhaps only rivaled by Christmas in terms of business generated—had been officially canceled by the prime minister for fear that thousands of people gathering on the streets and at parties would create a huge spike in COVID-19 infection rates. Consequently, all alcohol manufacturers, who would usually mount national campaigns, went silent.

I immediately saw an opportunity.

Carnival might not exist physically, as it did each year, but the spirit of revelry and joy—of what it meant to so many people—was still there, waiting to be tapped into.

My head of agency operations, Stacey Ryan, approached me with a piece of music she had heard that, in her opinion, struck that nostalgic chord we needed. She had that instinct for music, and the moment I heard the piece, I felt it.

The theme I developed was called "Hold On to the Carnival." The videos featured an empty street, reflecting the pandemic restrictions, with a single Carnival reveler. The scene then morphed into the same reveler in that identical location the year before. The street was packed with people dancing. This scene of desolation morphing into a nostalgic memory of the year before ran to the plaintive music, with the emotional plea of its chorus to "hold on to the carnival."

The response was unlike anything I could have expected. There was a huge outpouring of emotion on social media. It resonated widely. But the most significant impact was in the sales figures. The results defied all odds. Sales increased by 10.5 percent over the previous year when there was no pandemic. This completely reversed the client's projected 2.5 percent decline, despite impossible market conditions where consumption patterns had to change, as all bars and restaurants were closed and only carry-out service was being offered in a few locations.

What happened?

We literally struck a chord with consumers. We tapped into an emotional space and defied the physical limitations imposed by the restrictive regulations of COVID-19.

The Intangience Pillars of Purpose developed to deliver on the creative execution, insights, and strategy were along these lines:

- Who am I?

I am the relief and exuberance of Carnival.

- What is my purpose?

To provide you with that longed-for escape.

- How will I be remembered?

As a celebration of life.

- What is the Intangience insight?

We lose everything when hope is no longer there.

Notice how the beer became the embodiment of what people felt about the Carnival celebrations. Observe how the insight nudged the creative team to fully explore the idea of holding on.

PANDEMIC OF PERFORMANCE

The Carnival campaign was but one example of how we recorded a reversal of fortunes on the retail side during those challenging times. We also contributed significantly to guiding people through that emotionally troubling period with a campaign developed for a large wealth management and insurance firm called Guardian Group.

I'm a big believer in collaborative initiatives. Go to the world's best and enjoin them to deliver on the objectives.

Faced with circumstances in which people were fearful, depressed, isolated, and deeply uncertain about the future, this was the moment when leaders such as Guardian Group, who had served the region for more than 175 years, needed to guide us all through these times. I identified two areas that most needed addressing:

Emotional resilience: How could we best understand how to cope during the pandemic?

Innovation: How could we redefine our businesses and even renew outlooks to find opportunities amid the crisis?

I created two highly successful initiatives. The first was called Pandemic of Performance. The very title ironically suggested the turnaround inherent in the shifted perspective.

The initiative involved Richard Cox Braden of Stanford on innovation; Dr. Tal Ben-Shahar, best-selling author and former professor of positive psychology from Harvard; Dr. Guila Clara Kessous,[33] UNESCO Artist for Peace, on breaking free from self-imposed limits; Mohit Mukherjee,[34] founding director of the Centre for Executive Education of the UN's University for Peace, on a topic labeled "appreciative inquiry"; and me on Intangience and its ability to reframe challenges and identify new ways of connecting with yourself and others.

Over three thousand people participated in the online courses, which were run over three months. The testimonials were very touching, ranging from reports of saved relationships and emerging from depressive states to breakthroughs in business success. It was a timely intervention and one that was so sorely needed.

I recount this experience to reinforce to you the value of the Intangience principle stating that, often, approaching the emotional space first determines all other outcomes on every other level. The Pandemic of Performance became a process through which people saw things differently and became more resilient, hopeful, innovative, and confident in their ability not just to survive through difficult times but also to thrive through them.

---

33 Learn more about the profound Dr. Guila Kessous at https://turningpoint-leadership.com/coach/guila-clara-kessous/.

34 Read more about Mohit Mukherjee's remarkable background at https://fr.franklincovey.ca/engage-with-us/mohit-mukherjee/.

Happytalism

The Pandemic of Performance initiative was so successful that we followed it up with another, this one called Happytalism.[35] The Happytalism concept was initially developed by Jayme Illien and Luis Gallardo, who identified it as a new philosophy and economic system that promotes well-being and freedom at the center of all life. I loved their approach, the term *Happytalism*, and the way it conveyed the need to create both well-being and abundance in life.

I developed a free public initiative centered around Illien and Gallardo's inspiring theme of Happytalism. For this course, once more led by the iconic Dr. Tal Ben-Shahar, we registered more than four thousand participants from several countries and copped both the Gold and Best of Show Angel Awards for public service across the United States.

Let nothing deny you the ability to see an opportunity to move beyond any circumstance and challenge. They become nudges for greater understanding and growth.

When you acknowledge that you live in a world of intangibles, the power to change everything becomes clearer.

Remember the principle in the Science of Human Connection school of thought of Intangience called polyphonic understanding of the market. This is the ability to tune into current and emerging trends, attitudes, and behaviors.

My daughter, Lael-Anne, who was attending the United World College at the time, had me print buttons with no-handshake symbols to distribute to those attending a conference on happiness

35 Luis Gallardo, "Embracing Happytalism: A New Paradigm for Achieving Fundamental Peace - World Happiness Foundation," World Happiness Foundation (blog), May 28, 2024, https://worldhappiness.foundation/blog/community/embracing-happytalism-a-new-paradigm-for-achieving-fundamental-peace/.

in Costa Rica in early 2020, when we were just on the cusp of the pandemic. I recall resisting her insistence on handing these out to promote the protocol of no contact, physical spacing, and mask wearing at a time when it wasn't the norm. But she had been tracking the events emerging in Wuhan, China, and elsewhere. Within weeks of her cautions, the world had become familiar with the imposition of mask wearing and social distancing, along with a whole other host of restrictions and regulations.

When you acknowledge that you live in a world of intangibles, the power to change everything becomes clearer.

The same is true for just about any emerging event or trend that will impact large swaths of a localized or global population. Getting ahead of it all puts one in a position of significant advantage.

Seeking InvisAbility

Become a curiosity connoisseur and absorb the world around you from a global point of view. Search for reasons and answers. Question why things are happening. Apply the Intangience blueprint to these probes and you will begin to have what I call InvisAbility: the ability to perceive things not clear to others. Creativity is about the power of observation and the ability to create authentic human connections from it, whether through art, poetry, dance, or branding.

You might notice something in the intonation in someone's voice that helps you interpret how they are truly feeling. You might catch an expression in their eyes that reveals something else: a glimmer of sadness or anger or hurt or joy or curiosity. You might even notice it in someone's gait—the way they walk could tell you a story.

You may well ask what all of this has got to do with branding and business. It has everything to do with it. In the business context, it will allow you to scan the horizon for emerging trends and shifts in attitudes and consumer behavior. In interpersonal relationships, it will improve your understanding of people and yourself.

Allow me to tell you a story that unfolds the power of this.

One day, very early in my career, I received a call from an iconic businessman named Anthony Sabga.[36] A Syrian immigrant to Trinidad, he arrived at an early age with scarce resources. By the end of his illustrious life in his nineties, he had created one of the largest and most successful conglomerates in the region, with a presence in virtually every industry from energy to banking, media, construction, real estate, breweries, and more. The call surprised me on several levels. First of all, the call didn't come through an assistant. Instead, he was on the other end of the line.

"Hello, Ernie. Anthony Sabga here. How are you?" he asked cheerily, as though we had known each other for the longest while. I straightened in my seat, unsure of why this business titan would personally reach out to me. I fumbled through some polite reply that he cut short with a terse question: "Why don't you do any work for my Group?" he asked.

I could have offered a hundred reasons, but all I could stupidly muster up was that the advertising industry was run by a clique that made it difficult to even get accredited, much less grab the attention of a group as large as his.

"There are no cliques in my Group," Mr. Sabga curtly remarked.

"When can you come to see me, Ernie?" he asked. The warmth and charm had returned to his tone.

---

36 Dig deeper into Anthony Sabga's exceptional story at https://chamber.org.tt/wp-content/uploads/2016/06/2008-sabga.pdf.

I was dumbfounded. Mr. Sabga himself asking me when could I see him!

I felt like I was dreaming or someone was playing a cruel prank on me.

I replied that I was at his disposal and available to meet any time of any day.

I walked into his impressive office to meet him. He was dressed impeccably well in his three-piece pin-striped suit and brilliantly polished Italian leather shoes. His thick head of well-oiled black hair with streaks of gray was neatly brushed back. He stood up when I entered the room and walked briskly from behind his desk to warmly shake my hand.

To this day, I have only heard that the call from Mr. Sabga came through because he had seen some of my work for a bank and was impressed by the difference in my style. What I can say with certainty, though, is that it became one of the most influential meetings of my life. Mr. Sabga seemed to take an instant liking to me. He even had me attend various executive meetings, where he made me sit beside him. On many occasions, I was unsure why I was there, but he would always introduce me as someone who understood marketing. I'll skip over some of my most memorable interactions with this unusual, highly intelligent, and charismatic man who had the potential to explode in anger if things didn't go his way or if he felt misunderstood or challenged.

I learned to read Mr. Sabga's every mood, the nuances of his personality, and even his nonverbal habits. As an example, I discovered that he had a way of tapping his feet when he was becoming impatient. Those who pushed past this and pressed on with whatever they were saying, which he obviously disagreed with, would feel his wrath. The ironic thing was that he had a remarkable knack for being right. It was like he had some sixth sense for business, often going against the grain of the most expert opinions.

His confidence in me was sealed very early in our meetings when, sitting with key members of his marketing team from his CARIB Brewery, he snapped, "I want Carib to be like a red Solo and a roti." (This was a reference to a specific flavor of a local soft drink brand and a soft Indian flatbread that is hugely popular on the island.)

The red Solo soft drink had become so popular that people often referenced it together with roti, as in, "I'm feeling for a red Solo and a roti." The association between the soft drink brand and the culture of the island was what had caught the attention of Mr. Sabga.

I immediately saw the reaction of the Carib marketing team. Mr. Sabga had obviously been saying this for a while, and they wore perplexed and frustrated expressions, which he seemed to pick up on. He began to tap his feet, complaining bitterly that they were not following through on his instructions. I think it was more like they didn't understand what he meant. I was suddenly put on the spot when he turned angrily to look at me. However, his tone softened when he asked, "Ernie, what would you do?" It was my magical moment. I'm not quite sure where I gathered the inspiration from, but I just knew I understood precisely what he was asking for—to have the Carib brew seen as part of the social fabric of the island, an embodiment of who we were and the way we lived. I replied instantly with what was to become the script of one of the brand's popular TV spots.

I said, "It's in our eyes, the way we smile. It's in the way we walk, in the rhythm of our lives. It's in the games we play and the way we say the things we say. It's in the way we think and the beer we drink. Carib, identify yourself."

Mr. Sabga beamed and slapped his hand on the desk, startling everyone. He said, "That's it! How long would it take to produce it?"

And with that, I had earned my stripes and his confidence. I often ask myself how I got there, and I think the answer follows in what I want to share with you. It is called InvisAbility.

As part of your Intangience immersion, I ask you to join me in a course on InvisAbility.

If you happen to be in an office, on a bus, or in a public space, choose someone and, without them noticing, of course, observe them differently.

Before now, you might not have been aware of their physical presence. You might even have noticed very little about their appearance. How much of that person did you actually perceive? What might you have missed?

You can see invisibility in someone else's need to be noticed or acknowledged or hugged or fed or smiled at or helped in some way. Even highly successful and well-known people can feel as invisible as a homeless, hapless human being on the sidewalk.

Everywhere and anywhere, there is invisibility. Do you see sadness in another person's eyes? Do you hear joy in someone's voice? Do you feel another person's discomfort or sense their disconnection?

Invisibility lies in the ignored needs of others. Too often, we are blinded and desensitized. We are numbed and indifferent. We stumble through life, stepping over, around, and even on each other and everything, mindlessly, senselessly, and effortlessly oblivious to the beauty, the wonder, and the miracle that is life.

There will be times when you can detect that something is not right with someone without knowing how you came to that conclusion. Was it the sound of their voice, something in their eyes, the way they walked, stood, or sat, or even just the energy they carried with them?

Intangience Insights

Imagine being able to function at such a level—tuning into life at a frequency that picks up nuances and understanding, offering insights unseen by most. I genuinely believe that business visionaries such as Anthony Sabga develop this polyphonic understanding of the world, enabling them to quickly discern opportunities and evaluate market conditions through their curious minds. My own close personal and professional relationship with him grew by leaps and bounds as I deepened my understanding of him and learned to anticipate his thoughts and perspectives.

This principle applies in much the same way to your brand and its relationship with consumers. It's about understanding people just as much as it is about understanding the market.

If you don't go deeper into the reasons consumers buy your product or service, you won't really get the full cause-and-effect picture of the underlying reasons behind what will inspire customers to choose your brand.

Here's an example: Diamond sales spiked to record levels after the pandemic. Why? Couples were getting married in record numbers. (People were also getting divorced in record numbers, but that's a whole other story.) After two years of confinement, separation, and deferred weddings, people were clamoring for meaningful connections. So it was important in the midst of the pandemic to look ahead and predict how consumer behavioral patterns might shift.

But within that insight, there's something more.

A diamond is the least valuable gemstone in the world when compared to other gems. Its value came about when De Beers hired ad agency N. W. Ayer & Son in 1938 to create a campaign around this little-valued gem. "Diamonds are forever" (described by Ad Age as the most influential slogan of the century), and the gem's embodiment of love lingers to this day, giving the stone a meaning that connects to its intangible value and, in turn, its worth.

To connect a spike in diamond sales in a postpandemic world to the intangible value inherent in what the gem means to consumers and marriage is to understand how value and worth are created.

Are diamonds really forever?

As we apply the principle of tracking emerging trends and tuning into influences in consumer behavior, we are constantly required to update these analyses and opinions. While it is true that the demand for diamonds saw a surge after the pandemic, it is equally true today that there is currently the biggest challenge to the dominance of minerally acquired diamonds.

Who would have thought this level of challenge would have been possible just a few years ago, unless one were tracking the undercurrents of the industry? There is ever-growing concern about the ethics of the diamond industry, relative to immoral labor practices including exploitation of children, the environment, and the proceeds being used to fund civil wars. "Ethical sourcing" the likes of which lab diamonds can claim would obviously help to raise the conscience-driven, guilt-free alternative. Improvements in the technology that today produces a diamond that is indistinguishable from natural ones at a fraction of the cost now make for a compelling choice.[37]

In 2024, 52 percent of couples surveyed said their engagement ring featured a lab-grown diamond according to the 2025 Real

37 Gary Simpson, "When Did Lab Grown Diamonds Become Popular: Tracing the Rise in Demand," Diamondrensu, February 26, 2024, https://diamondrensu.com/blogs/lab-grown-diamonds/when-did-lab-grown-diamonds-become-popular.

Weddings Study by The Knot.[38] But here is an interesting point: With the increased demand for lab-grown diamonds, prices are predicted to continue dropping substantially, causing an article by *The Economist* to quote, "If, as seems likely, lab grown lose their signalling value, a much steeper fall in prices is in store." It added, "Although a boyfriend might be happy to take a chance on a $4,000 larger lab grown diamond rather than a $6,000 smaller, natural stone, he will probably turn up his nose at a $300 dollar ring compared with a $6,000 one. Nobody wants to be that cheap a husband."[39] This is a dramatic reinforcement of the whole intangible.

So what would the Intangience approach be to this?

If we represented De Beers, we would pose the question in our advertising as to whether a suitor wanted to show their Real Love or choose the cheaper route in expressing the depth of their dedication and commitment (which is the embodiment of what, in reality, isn't at all the most precious gem). Show Her the Real Love would be switching the persuasion into the emotional space, with the expression of love being only real with a natural diamond as opposed to one produced in a lab.

On the other hand, if Intangience is applied to the lab diamond industry, we would pose the question as to whether the suitor wanted to show True Love or choose the "unethically sourced mined diamond" that exploits people and the environment and promotes war as an inappropriate expression of what should really symbolize true love. Again, the pivotal point would be to craft the message emotionally through shared intangible values. Ironically, the very idea of the

38 "What 2025 Couples Should Know About The Knot Real Wedding Study," The Knot, February 26, 2025, https://www.theknot.com/content/wedding-data-insights/real-weddings-study.

39 "Don't Propose with a Diamond," *The Economist*, February 26, 2025, https://www.economist.com/finance-and-economics/2025/02/06/dont-propose-with-a-diamond.

diamond itself is an intangible value given worth through what it represents as a symbol of love and commitment.

Remember, meaning is at the heart of all relationships. In the absence of meaning, there is no value placed upon anything, be it a physical asset or a human relationship. What are the hidden meanings behind the insights you gather about your brand's connection to your consumers?

That's part of our reframing the world around and within ourselves. To see things differently. To recognize the intangible and know how to transform it all into something meaningful and valuable.

Intangience Inquiries

1. How can you begin to develop your InvisAbility?
2. What outcomes are you hoping for as you intentionally increase your perception of the people and life around you?
3. What is a polyphonic understanding of the market, and how does it connect to the core principles of InvisAbility?
4. Why was the beer company's campaign "Hold On to the Carnival" able to resonate so deeply that it reversed anticipated declines amid the pandemic lockdowns, bar closures, and declining disposable income?
5. Why did the public initiatives Pandemic of Performance and Happytalism work so well?

INTANGIENCE
INTANGIENCE
INTANGIENCE
INTANGIENCE
INTANGIENCE
INTANGIENCE
INTANGIENCE
INTANGIENCE
INTANGIENCE
INTANGIENCE
INTANGIENCE

CHAPTER EIGHT

HOW TO SELL A BANANA AND DUCT TAPE FOR $6.2 MILLION

Money often costs too much.

—RALPH WALDO EMERSON[40]

I was surprised when I received an unscheduled call from one of the most highly regarded executives of a major regional bank group. It was very early in my career, and I had yet to build any kind of reputation worthy of receiving the attention of someone as influential as he was, much less to be then given the opportunity that occasioned it.

"I have an opportunity for you to make a name for yourself," he told me matter-of-factly. "We bought out this bank, but we're receiving a lot of bad press, and it's affecting the bank's performance. Your job is to build a public relations campaign to answer the questions troubling customers about the takeover."

40 Ralph Waldo Emerson, "Wealth," Essay, *Essays and English Traits* (P.F. Collier & Son, 1909).

I later discovered that this was a significant understatement of the challenge I faced. The bank that had been bought by this group was the National Commercial Bank of Grenada. If we didn't turn around the bank's fortunes within a few months at most, there could be a run on it that would devastate the bank and impact Grenada's economy. At the same time, an entire national community resisted the bank's acquisition by its new foreign owners. The media was having a field day with this acquisition of Grenada's national bank by a large foreign bank for what was being reported as a paltry sum. The criticism was that the bank had sold out the national patrimony.

This was more than just "bad press," as the executive had described it. This was a virtual revolt. The tension was so bad that employees of the bank—who were all local—were being harassed on the street when seen wearing their uniforms!

What could we possibly do?

"We don't have much of a budget for the campaign," the bank executive had told me. "If you're interested, you will have to pay for your own airfare, accommodations, and other expenses."

Even at that stage of my career, this seemed grossly unfair, but he must have recognized that I would relish the opportunity to serve the needs of this large financial institution and prove myself. So, I took out a loan (from another bank, as I didn't want to reveal my financial desperation to this new client) and flew over to meet with the senior team of the acquired bank.

I soon realized that there was no way to quell the anger and resentment felt by all and sundry, including even some of the bank's employees. The proposed question-and-answer public relations releases would only embolden the critics and exacerbate the situation. Calls for boycotting the bank were already taking root, and if the situation got any worse, there would be a run on the bank.

I took the opportunity while on the picturesque island of Grenada to discover everything I could about the place. I found out what Grenadians were proud of and passionate about—the things that made the island both unique and famous. In short, I did a "how to become a Grenadian in twenty-four hours" immersion course.

I left there with a better understanding of who these friendly, fiercely nationalistic people were. I called the bank executive and explained my findings. Simply put, no amount of so-called public relations strategies trying to rationalize the takeover of the local bank would work. Trying to explain how the valuation of the price was arrived at or even how good this would be for Grenada and Grenadians would be vacuous. In fact, it would feed the story and further inflame an already highly emotionally charged debate.

What I sought to do instead was to integrate the most proudly nationalistic communication ever seen:

We began by determining that our public relations campaign would feature the Grenada dove, a species of bird only found on that island.

Next, we hired Junior Murray, the first cricketer of Grenada ever selected for the regional West Indies team, as our spokesperson.

We sponsored a netball tournament and asked Grenadians to create a catchy song about the great things that were happening in Grenada.

We launched a campaign themed "Time Is Money" that addressed the fastest loan processing application on the island, responding to an issue that had been a source of significant customer frustration.

We introduced the island's first ATM in a celebratory ceremony even though we were at least six months behind our competitors. Going to market first with the launch and not the service helped validate the benefits customers would derive.

At the end of it all, we shifted the conversation from who owned the bank to showcasing the institution to be more Grenadian than ever before and run by Grenadians for a better Grenada.

The bank not only grew by leaps and bounds, but to this day, it is one of the premier financial institutions on the island.

Focus on Feelings

The important takeaway from this is that it is yet another example of how feelings count for more than facts. We connect more emotionally. Our decisions are driven more by our feelings than by logic and intellect.

If you don't understand and develop the language of human connection, you may not succeed in getting your message through as intended. Communicating in the same language isn't quite the same as sharing the same intangible values and being engaged on an emotional level.

Even the value and very idea of money aren't as tangible as you might think.

The economist Bernard Lietaer defines money as "an agreement to use something standardized as a medium of exchange within a community."[41] A good example of the *intangible* value of money is that it is a means to an end—that is, the whole ideal of money having a direct value relationship with what

If you don't understand and develop the language of human connection, you may not succeed in getting your message through as intended.

41 "Rethinking the Concept of Money," Austen Morris Associates, https://www.austen-morris.com/rethinking-the-concept-of-money/.

an individual deeply desires to do with it and the ability of the money to be so used.

The value of money to someone is determined by the meaning it has relative to what the individual requires or chooses to do with it in the context of its ability to satisfy needs and achieve goals.

This is critical in understanding to what extent someone will look to acquire and deploy monetary resources when they are persuaded or dictated by the need to acquire something, whether tangible or intangible. It's not the money that is the commodity but the extent to which an individual decides that what it can provide is something they deeply need.

In this sense, the commodity becomes the desire and need, and money is simply a common agreement of exchange toward allowing the trade to be completed. The value, therefore, is determined by an intangible.

A further explanation of the concept of money can be derived from Joseph Schumpeter, Austrian finance minister and political economist, who described money as a "claim ticket"[42] to goods or commodities rather than as a commodity itself.

In summary, in the absence of money being able to satisfy a need or goal, it holds no meaning and, therefore, no value. If you were to keenly understand this approach to money, it would alter how you attributed value to any offering.

---

42 Cited by Agnès Festré and Eric Nasica, "Schumpeter on Money, Banking, and Finance: An Institutionalist Perspective," *European Journal of the History of Economic Thought* 16, no. 2 (2009): 325–356, https://shs.hal.science/halshs-00272405v1/document.

The Value of Art

You might be familiar with the so-called art piece by Maurizio Cattelan called *Comedian*, which is nothing more than a banana affixed to a wall with a piece of duct tape. When first sold in 2019, it fetched a price of $120,000. Five years later, at a Sotheby's auction, the piece (with a new banana, of course) sold for an astonishing $6.2 million.[43]

The artwork comes with instructions on how to install the tape and the banana. I guess *Comedian* is about the artist having the last laugh!

However, Cattelan has said that his artwork is not intended as a joke. Instead, he describes it as "a sincere commentary and a reflection on what we value."[44] A fellow artist, a Georgian performance artist, created his own artistic interpretation when *Comedian* was displayed at the Art Basel Miami Beach art fair in 2019. In a performance piece he titled *Hungry Artist*, he removed the banana and ate it. Indeed, Justin Sun—the Chinese cryptocurrency entrepreneur who paid $6.2 million for *Comedian*—reportedly also planned to eat the banana after the acquisition.[45]

---

43 Nate Freeman, "The $6.2 Million Banana, Explained," *Vanity Fair*, Nov. 22, 2024, https://www.vanityfair.com/style/story/maurizio-cattelan-banana-explained?srsltid=AfmBOooD9anDN6rOCY2AODZTEDFENUrfrtsOgbCLsrqaqh-vsDUQw2xO.

44 Tanya Ott, "Why a Duct-Taped Banana Sold for Millions of Dollars," DW, November 21, 2024, https://www.dw.com/en/why-a-duct-taped-banana-sold-for-millions-of-dollars/a-70754311.

45 Ibid.

SOMETHING ONLY HAS VALUE...

...WHEN IT HOLDS MEANING.

This is all so reminiscent to me of the folktale "The Emperor's New Clothes" by Danish author Hans Christian Andersen. It's about a vain emperor who is tricked into thinking he is wearing garb that can only be seen by the very wise, resulting in him exposing himself naked before his subjects.

What is of most significance is that the value of this "art installation" is essentially established by whatever meaning is ascribed to it.

This is perhaps akin to a famous "musical" piece by John Cage titled *4'33"*. It was composed in 1952 for any instrument or a combination of instruments, and it is divided into three movements lasting, respectively, thirty seconds, two minutes and twenty-three seconds, and one minute and forty seconds.

The score specifically instructs performers *not* to play their instruments throughout the three movements, so for the four minutes and thirty-three seconds that the composition lasts, there is only silence, broken by the occasional ambient sound. This experience of silence and background noise is purposefully designed to contribute to the performance.

As you might imagine, when *4'33"* was first introduced, it was received with shock and confusion, all leading to quite a controversy. Music historian James Pritchett describes what he calls "the silent piece" as "more a means than an end, a mental, spiritual, and compositional exercise. Its literal silence reflects the silence of the will necessary to open up a realm of infinite possibilities."[46]

Now whatever your interpretation or understanding of the silent piece, which has been "performed" many times, the question is "What was it that created value or worth to the idea of attending a concert in which people knew ahead of time that no musical instrument would be heard or played?"

I put it to you that it was because of the regard with which the composer was held, much like the value attributed to the *Comedian* banana–duct tape art installation of Maurizio Catellan. It was the reputation of those talented individuals that created the value and worth of these two works of art.

Intangience Insights

This brings us back to the meaning of things and the corresponding value attached to them—a clear reminder of the Intangience principle that something only has *value* when it holds *meaning* for those who seek to possess it.

The value of *Comedian* and *4'33"*—two admittedly extreme examples—demonstrates that the works of these two individuals had a preset meaning. Their very names translated into a presumption of a value set. In the same way, a painting without the signature of the artist can be expected to be worth considerably less than if it were

46 James Pritchett, *The Music of John Cage* (Cambridge University Press, 1996), 60.

signed. The signature itself gives it authenticity and validates the piece. It's all intangible value ascribed through meaning.

Life itself is a search for meaning, without which concepts of happiness and contentment become more elusive than ever. So, from a personal and professional perspective, we will grow and expand our moments here best when we understand how much this informs everything about ourselves and the world in which we live.

Intangience Inquiries

1. What made the banana and duct tape art installation by Maurizio Cattelan fetch a price of $6.2 million?
2. What intangible value gives money its worth?
3. Why is the *4'33"* composition by John Cage so highly regarded?

INTANGIENCE

INTANGIENCE
INTANGIENCE
INTANGIENCE
INTANGIENCE
INTANGIENCE
INTANGIENCE
INTANGIENCE
INTANGIENCE
INTANGIENCE
INTANGIENCE

CHAPTER NINE

HOW TO REDEFINE AND REFRAME EVERYTHING TO DISCOVER THE RIGHT ANSWER

The formulation of a problem is often more essential than its solution.

—ALBERT EINSTEIN[47]

As we come closer to the conclusion of this insightful experience, I think it might be good to share a piece from my course on creativity. When I first created it, I thought it was such a novel approach, but I have since found that others also use this question to nudge the imaginative process.

It's called "What if?" It's a way to inspire reflection and insights with a simple question: What if? It's an invitation—an act of encouragement to push beyond ordinary framing and expectations and examine the world in a fresh and new way.

Let's see how this works in practice by considering how asking this question might have inspired some of the world's leading brands to create innovative identities and messages.

47 Albert Einstein and Leopold Infeld, *Evolution of Physics* (Cambridge Univ. Press, 1958).

Maybe this approach helped nudge Coca-Cola to become an embodiment of happiness and human connection. What if a bottle of this sugary liquid contained the spirit of joy and human connection? *Open happiness.*

Maybe it aided Nike to become an embodiment of personal aspiration and motivation. What if this sneaker were more than just foam, fabric, and rubber? What if it could move us to believe in ourselves and inspire us to achieve big goals, no matter how impossible they seem? *Just do it.*

Maybe it made Louis Vuitton an embodiment of power, affluence, and exclusive works of art. What if these were more than just bags made of fabric and leather stitched together in factories around the world, from China to the US? What if this were the best way to move first class through life on an adventure of exclusivity? *The art of travel.*

Maybe all of the creators of these brands asked a fundamental question: If this weren't a bottle of sugary liquid/a sneaker/a handbag, what could it mean to people emotionally?

Ask yourself this same what-if question. What if your brand were to be seen as an object of desire *emotionally*? What could it be?

Suspend rationality. Don't overthink the exercise. Have fun with the craziness that might emerge. The point of all this is that, in the emotional space, feelings can take us anywhere and for all kinds of unreasonable reasons.

The Color of Connection

When product or service offerings become contained in emotions, you can land just about anywhere in this playful pursuit of pleasurable feelings by drawing from a wide palate of colorful human connections. Think of the many memorable campaigns of major brands and you will see the way they communicate on these deeply emotional levels through compelling stories based upon the intangible values embodied by those brands.

We encounter and experience the world around us in very individual ways. The reality of it all is based upon how we're interpreting it.

Take color as an example. No one sees color in quite the same way. It's interpreted through individual experience. In some parts of the world, there is even a heightened awareness of more hues of color based upon words that exist to describe these nuances of difference.

Perhaps this helps explain why, as limitless as our imagination might be, we simply cannot imagine a wholly new color. Just try thinking of an entirely new color—one that doesn't currently exist. It simply isn't possible.

The old question of whether a tree that falls in the forest makes a sound if no one is there to hear it can scientifically be answered by a definitive no. The tree falling makes no sound, other than the vibrations created by the fall. When those vibrations enter our ears, they are translated by our brains into a sound.

All of this is to reinforce the point that the world is encountered through interpretation by our senses and further by experiences, cultures, belief systems, and a host of other factors. Once we understand the complexity of this, we are better able to appreciate what presumptive reality is to us. This presumptive reality is that in which we *presume* things to be, creating an understanding of reality that is unique to each individual.

As limitless as our imagination might be, we simply cannot imagine a wholly new color.

When you create authentic connections with someone else, you're entering their version of reality by accurately or effectively helping them to perceive things as *you* intend based upon *their* intangible values, perceptions, and interpretations. That's a powerful level of persuasion or influence that can—of course—be negative or positive. Even deciding whether the outcome is positive or not is itself an interpretation.

It becomes clear why there's a critical need to speak the language of human connection. In order to connect authentically, you need to recognize the power of intangible values and the very human perceptions that shape them.

The Challenge of Shifting Perspectives

In the Intangience courses, I use a series of thought-provoking challenges to teach participants how to shift their perspective. One of these ("How would you sell a used toothbrush?") we considered in chapter 2. But I find it incredibly helpful to engage in the work of seeing the world through different lenses, and I invite you to consider your answers to these questions:

- How would you help someone who was born blind to understand color?
- If happiness were a sound or a color or a face or a place, what would each of these be to you?
- If you had to create a thirty-second TV ad for a seat belt without using words or images of the seat belt or its benefits (including crashed cars or injured people), how would you achieve this?
- If a foreign beer entered your local market, offering comparative quality at a much lower price, and every discount and promotion created so far had failed, what would you do?

Each of these exercises causes you to think differently. The questions force you to contemplate a challenge or answer a question through its framing. Many of the answers will come only by being emotionally engaged in creating appropriate and accurate answers. They will also compel you to apply the techniques and devices that help you connect at another level.

Making this kind of thinking a practice will help in expanding your understanding of the most complex of situations and challenges.

You will find yourself readily adopting a larger perspective on things and being able to interpret challenges differently.

Let's try one more challenge—this time exploring how this process can redefine marketing in the world of business.

Suppose that we are going to invest in a flower farm together, and we've decided to specialize in roses. Let's say we have managed to get all the fundamentals right. We've calculated all the costs and processes: the cost of the land, seeds, fertilizers; the threats to growth; labor; and the shipment of the flowers under temperature-controlled conditions to maintain freshness and quality. Every detail has been considered.

However, if we ignore one intangible value, we're missing out on a crucial detail of the business.

What is the point in time during the calendar year when the roses will be valued and worth significantly more than at any other? More specifically, what *day* will the roses carry a higher price and be more sought after—a day so significant that if they arrive one day later, their value is significantly less?

That day, of course, is Valentine's Day.

Try sending your valentine roses on February 15 instead of February 14. It's certain that your loved one will be unhappy, unless you have a really good reason for their deferred arrival!

The intangible value of a rose as an expression of love is what determines its worth on Valentine's Day. It's not so much the flower itself as what it means and represents on that day.

But let's reflect even further on this. It completely alters the definition of the business we're in when we explore the industry through the lens of the relevant intangible values.

Let's look beyond Valentine's Day to other days when flowers are sold. When are flowers usually shared with another person? It could be to express love or congratulations or an apology, or even condolences.

So, if we consider flowers using the Intangience interpretation of an industry of human relationship, what might they be? Suddenly, you're not simply in the floral industry. You could better define your industry as being in the business of human acknowledgment—people acknowledging each other through the gifting and sharing of things such as flowers.

Now you can develop the business further through this insight. You understand what is driving the purchase. Yes, the flowers' quality, price, and distribution and all the other fundamentals of business are important, but you're not going to compete well enough or successfully persuade your customer until you understand what is emotionally driving that value and creating that conviction.

Understanding now that you're in the *acknowledgment* business will help you ensure that you bring that into your company culture and brand. It might even cause you to add other items that people use to acknowledge each other in simple ways, such as boxes of chocolates, specialty cards, and even personalized songs composed through an app offered by your store to accompany any range of thoughtful messages.

Intangience Insights

This is how you separate your brand from that of your competitors with more than just price and quality. You're redefining your business to better reflect the emotional space that you occupy.

It's yet another example of how important intangibles are in the world of business and marketing.

I once won a pizza account by asking the client to pick his worst day of the year and give me the opportunity to make it his best. He accepted the challenge.

My agency created National Pizza Day long before it became known internationally. The results were overwhelming. To this day, the brand owns that space on the date my client identified as typically having their lowest sales, June 18, and the client reports that it has sustained a high point of success. An intangible celebration transformed the sales point from lowest to highest.

We worked with another client in the same industry, Pizza Hut, to discover that there was a correlation between heavy rainy days and high sales. Digging deeper into the data, we guessed that more customers were coming into the outlets because of the weather, and developed a campaign to further drive this sales spike.

Our campaign was built around a clear message: "When it rains, it pours with savings at Pizza Hut!"

This theme was activated on days of heavy rainfall, offering specials, as we learned that traffic congestion created by the weather encouraged customers to pick up a meal to take home or eat on the way. Had we not been tracking the intangibles, we might never have spotted this trend or known how to take advantage of it through the right messaging.

Let's take one last look at the what-if process and our flower business. Since we redefined the business as being in the acknowledgment industry of human relationships, we could now expand our offering.

What if we didn't think of our product as flowers to convey sentiments? What if they were birds of love like trained homing pigeons carrying messages taped to their legs to specific locations? (There is actually a business, PigeonGram, that does this!) What if we added singing telegrams to our flower deliveries? What if we made flower deliveries even easier by using Uber?

The *what if* nudges you in an endless flow to create what you might not have thought possible before.

Enjoy the flight of fancy to wherever the world of intangibles takes you.

Intangience Inquiries

1. What does it mean to see a business through the lens of an industry of human relationship?
2. What is presumptive reality?
3. Using the what-if process, how could you develop a new message to define your personal or professional brand?

CHAPTER TEN

HOW IT ALL STARTED

The purpose of life is a life of purpose.

—ROBERT BYRNE

Let's conclude this final chapter on Intangience by going back to how it all started: my quest to find meaning in my life.

At a point in my life when I had achieved many of my biggest goals, I still felt lost. I had built a successful advertising and branding agency from nothing. I had arrived penniless in a country where I knew no one and built a broad network of accomplished leaders and a financially rewarding career. My agency had just received an accolade as the most awarded agency in the region. Clients were rushing through our doors.

Professionally, I had hit every touchpoint of success I had set for myself.

On a personal level, I had raised my daughter largely on my own, and she had grown into a bright, value-centered, beautiful human being—the greatest of all my achievements.

Yet I felt unfulfilled and purposeless. I recognized that it was frustrating, even ungrateful, of me to feel this way, but I just couldn't shake the deep sense of nothingness and futility.

I shared how I felt with a friend of mine. I expressed my fear that I wasn't even sure that I was leaving enough materially for my daughter.

My friend told me something that I've never forgotten. She replied, "It isn't what you leave *for* her. It's what you're leaving *with* her."

It was an epiphanic moment in my life. Her words stung. They also rang deeply, uncomfortably true.

What indeed was I leaving with my daughter and the world? How had I contributed to making a difference for her and others because I had lived?

While I had always comforted myself that my charitable nature was a quality of character that defined me as a good person, it surely couldn't be enough to be considered a legacy.

I was inspired to take action. I followed through by doing two things. The first was that I established a philanthropic organization called ReThink dedicated to promoting kindness and well-being using the very techniques we had successfully deployed for clients to create engagement and shareability for their messages. This would later grow into a full-fledged registered NGO thanks to one of our creative directors and the resource lead at ReThink, Chester Parris. Chester helped launch an initiative called Band of Support, an online resource that connected individuals and families in need with people who were willing to donate their time and expertise for everything from home repair services and professional counseling to books, clothing, or groceries. ReThink became very well known as a leader in the kindness and happiness space and for the novel way we promoted it.

The second thing I did to fill the void was to create a personal development methodology based upon my successful approaches in the world of advertising. Initially, my intent was for this work to simply be an opportunity to build my capacity for the kind of personal reflection and introspection that might help me work through my feelings of worthlessness.

Thus, Intangience was born.

I shared the process with others and discovered how impactful it was in bringing clarity and defining a life of greater purpose and meaning. So, I developed an event at a park in collaboration with a major conglomerate. It was called The Gift and promised to deliver crucial answers for a life of happiness.

The event attracted hundreds of people to enjoy musical performances and an insightful video, also titled *The Gift*.

The impact of this intervention made me realize how much of my unique approach to branding development was being applied to this very personal work. I was nudged to take the process further into a full-fledged branding methodology based upon my award-winning work in the field. Encouraged by one of my dearest friends, an inspirational genius on so many levels and my mentor, Heidi Achong, to develop Intangience on a global scale, I ended up in Costa Rica, where the United Nations–established University for Peace is located. There, I met the founding director of the Centre for Executive Education, Mohit Mukherjee—a brilliant, generous soul who guided me on how to create training modules out of my methodology. He also gave me the opportunity to present Intangience to a group of professors and others from the center. These leaders decided to certify the methodology for inclusion in their educational program.

All of a sudden, I had a UN-certified branding and entrepreneurial development methodology, which allowed me to share each of the key steps in the language and science of human connection. Within months, through several collaborations, over ten thousand participants in various countries had been guided through the course. Captains of industry and professors from leading learning institutions such as Harvard gave flattering testimonies to its impact and innovations.

I realized that many people were telling me how much they gained from the immersion on both a professional and personal level. It reminded me of how it all started from my own yearning for meaning.

The Personal Illumination

So, as I often do at the close of my courses on branding, I will conclude this final chapter on what may be the most important session of all in your Intangience immersion.

It is about how to apply the principles to your personal life.

The businesses and brands you develop shouldn't be divorced from your own identity, purpose, and values. Let's take this opportunity to apply the Intangience process to you personally.

As we mentioned earlier in the book, the three introspective probes of the Pillars of Purpose are the most important you can ever pose to yourself:

- Who am I?
- What is my purpose?
- How will I be remembered?

In much the same way as you applied these to the development of your brand identity and message, you can use the same process in an intentional self-introspection.

- Who am I?

Think beyond your name, your career, and the various roles you play in life and beyond being a father or mother, brother or sister, friend, spouse, employee, or manager. Move past all of that. Beyond your nationality, your ethnicity, your culture, your religious or political or other beliefs.

Who are you?

Consider who you are when you are not defined by anyone else's expectations and demands. Strip away everything that usually defines you so you're left only with the contemplation of the core of your true character—the person you truly are at heart.

This essence is much more than just your identity. This is an opportunity to explore what truly defines you as a person. Search for answers that express your true self. Find that authentic voice that acknowledges you. Let your uniqueness soar. Discover the essence of yourself. Encounter the epiphany of knowing who you truly happen to be.

Write as clearly and concisely and as honestly as you possibly can: I am …

The next level equips you to recognize and understand why you're here at all. Life can't just be about the various roles we play.

- What is my purpose?

Once again, resist the traditional boundaries of roles and titles. Look beyond the purpose you fulfill as a family member, a business associate, a friend, or any other role you play.

What might be a deeper purpose you can identify for your presence here on earth? Is there some deeper contribution that nudges you?

Consider a purpose greater than yourself—something that you believe is crucially important. What might that be?

Now, visualize yourself playing that role.

This then brings you to the retrospective point in the process. It is the point at which you have the gift of looking back at the life you've lived and consider what legacy might have been left.

- How will I be remembered?

Here, you're not measuring academic or material achievements. Instead, you're identifying how you might measure the impact your words, your actions, and your very self have made upon the lives of others. What lasting, meaningful difference did your life create?

Challenge yourself to look within.

Do this not from a posture of fear or anxiety. Instead, choose curiosity. Have a sense of adventure about meeting yourself in this new way.

Embrace this opportunity to discover what truly defines you as a human being and to identify with joy the greater purpose for which you were born.

So far, the process has been largely about you and your relationship with the world.

Now it's time to elevate it to legacy and to understand the way in which others will look at your life and how you lived. This part of your personal geography is about finding the lasting footprints observed fondly by others as you journeyed through and around their lives. How did you touch them? What lasting impression and difference did you make?

Who did you become to others?

This is your bookmark. It marks the page to which people can turn—that particular page upon which your life is indelibly recorded. It is a collection of every moment you have shared with everyone on the planet during your lifetime. It is a scrapbook of memories. It is a telling account of the person you happen to be.

It is ultimately the way you will always be remembered.

Expand your mind to get there. Move beyond yourself. Travel outside to experience others encountering you.

This requires absolute clarity of perspective. More than an out-of-body experience, it is actually an experience in another's body, looking back at all of your life's key encounters as you try to realize the impact you might have made upon others as you explore the question, "How will I be remembered?"

You're not simply analyzing potential areas of impact. You're embarking on a journey to reset your life. You're intentionally choosing to look back and assess where, how, and why your life will make a positive difference to the world and those around you, shaping a legacy of true meaning.

Intangience Insights

As always, we end by seeking to answer the question, "What is the Intangience insight?" This time, we're seeking a significant aha moment—an epiphanic understanding from the process.

So, I ask with hope and great compassion: Which universal truth, what profound insight might have emerged from this for you?

What holds true from this introspection that can guide your future direction?

What have you learned about yourself and your reason for being alive now, in this moment?

The answer that emerges must feel like a moment of epiphany. You must recognize the very reason why *you*, uniquely, were born.

When the dance of this pursuit traces the pattern of your existence, the code of your soul is unlocked, and you recognize it immediately.

That's who I am. That's what I'm about. That's why I'm here!

Then we arrive at the phase I define as the Currency of Connection.

It is the way in which the life you live and the person you have chosen to become connects with others so powerfully that it ignites a positive chain reaction. You are now a channel of change—a magnet of positivity constantly touching lives in a way that causes them, in turn, to touch others.

You can expand on this understanding using the now-familiar three *R*s:

- Relevance: What is it about your life that is of real relevance to others? Again, this relevance is not found in the usual roles you play but applies even to strangers. Here, you're exploring how much your life might be of greater relevance to your community, your country, and even the world, in a way that people seek you out or light up when you are around.
- Regard: How do people regard you? Once more, I challenge you to look beyond your achievements and consider more than the usual definitions you might use, such as employer or provider. How are your values being manifested in your life? Are they impacting others in such a way that they have a high regard for how you show up positively in their lives?
- Resonance: Are you in touch with what deeply matters to others? Do people respond well to that connection? Do you understand their perspectives and needs and are you contributing in remarkable ways to them?

Finally, we are at the Intangience stage defined as the Science of Human Connection. Again, the three principles apply.

To connect to a life well lived, there must be a purpose that wakes you up each morning. Not the usual routines but something much more significant within you. Something that is so fulfilling and rewarding that it cannot be quantified monetarily. It's that discovery of what drives you—the source of energy so powerful that there is nothing more important in your life.

- Purpose: What purpose might you be living every day in service of a truly fulfilling life? It doesn't have to be grand, but it must be deeply meaningful to you.
- Passion: What is it about your life that everyone encounters and recognizes—the drive that brings you the most pleasure? It is important to note here that this motivation doesn't have to be altruistic or focused exclusively on serving others. It is, quite simply, the thing that you feel so fulfilled by that you can't imagine not doing it.
- Polyphonic understanding: How are you tuning into all that is affecting the world around you? Are you learning to listen intently to the sound of someone's voice or the environment around you? Are you practicing mindfulness? Do you embrace the joy of simply being alive to everything and filled with gratitude for it all? Are you listening to others intently? Are you truly observing the world in which you live? Are you identifying the needs of others?

The ability to tune into all creates the opportunity for true revelation. With such keen awareness, you begin to acknowledge and experience an abundant life.

The Universal Language

I'd like to end by sharing a beautiful dream I had while deeply immersed in the Intangience introspection.

It is the story of an accomplished musical composer who is blind and a renowned artist who happens to be deaf. They fall madly in love with each other.

Contemplate this for a moment.

This composer who is blind writes the most beautiful music and compositions that are revered around the world. It's almost as if the loss of his sight has given him a heightened awareness of spiritual vibrations—a gift that he expresses through music that deeply touches others.

His love, an amazing artist who happens to be deaf, has the ability to create stunning masterpieces. She is widely regarded as a maestro. It's as if her inability to hear has opened up another dimension of communication and perception of the world around her.

They are deeply in love with each other.

While he will never see the hues and images of her stunning works of art and she will never hear a note of his magical musical compositions, they can still understand, connect, and discover who they truly are at the heart of it all beyond their limitations. Unable to share each other's gifts, they find ways to connect. They are able to discover something more profound: each other's true value and worth.

We might not adequately discover the deepest truths about the mysteries of life even as we pursue answers to the questions of why we're here, what happens when we die, and what impact our lives will have. But the limitations of this human experience can't deny us the beauty and purpose we can encounter now. Much like the two accomplished and gifted artists in the story, we can live beyond the limitations that might cause us to feel disconnected from the best in each other and find that gift of a life that is abundant in love.

Perhaps the answers to age-old questions about the meaning of life—why we're here and how we can leverage our sense of purpose and passion for meaningful impact—cannot be truly understood because they exist in a language that we, as humans, cannot understand until we no longer exist as we do now.

But while we *are* here in the flesh, there are certain fundamental truths that we can grasp. We can understand that our lives are more intangible than we realize.

If nothing from nothing is an irrefutable law of physics, then what could possibly have *first* existed before everything else?

In the beginning, everything was entirely intangible.

This is a profound insight into the question of what *first* existed.

Throughout this book, we have demonstrated how real and powerful the very notion of intangibles are in so many spheres of life. So we should have a deep appreciation of how something that can't be held, weighed, or shipped still exists and causes the manifestation of many other things tangibly. We have learned as well that reality is entirely based upon an interpretation of what we perceive and how shifts in perspectives can alter things. In the recognition of the intangible world in which we live lies the answer to everything—the immeasurable, unquantifiable, unseen but undeniable existence of nothing from which everything emerged.

We can also recognize that there can be no greater meaning than when you discover that pure, unconditional love is what defines a life of purpose. It is the most powerful of intangibles and liberating of truths.

As you end this book, my hope is that you have found gems to take away—knowledge that will help you to "do well and do good" in life, as Dr. Tal Ben-Shahar advocates.

Please use these insights with good intentions and reap life's richest rewards through them. Live the life you were meant to live—one that is filled with meaning and purpose. You have now learned the language of human connection, and your life story will be best written through your understanding of it all.

INTANGIENC
INTANGIENC
INTANGIENC
INTANGIENC
INTANGIENC
INTANGIENC
INTANGIENC
INTANGIENC
INTANGIENC
INTANGIENC
INTANGIENC

EPILOGUE

Use these as reminders of what you've learned in the preceding pages—a summary of the Intangience insights that will guide you in your professional and personal life:

- Who am I?

I am a profound insight into that which connects us all.

- What is my purpose?

To create positive shifts in perspective.

- How will I be remembered?

As a channel through which I can understand what matters most to others.

- What is the Intangience insight?

Something only has value when it holds meaning for those who seek to possess it.

How do I create the Currency of Conversation?

By ensuring that the message is relevant to my audience and is shared through a community or spokesperson who is held in high regard, and that the content resonates deeply on a personal level.

- How will I apply the Science of Human Connection?

By defining how the message reflects a greater purpose based upon those intangible values that are so deeply important to my audience that it ignites a passion about what is shared. Key to all of this is recognizing that I must first develop a polyphonic understanding of what is influencing current and emerging trends, behaviors, beliefs, and opinions and then use that understanding to craft a meaningful message.

Ten Intangience Insights

1. Something only has value when it holds meaning to those who seek to possess it.
2. A brand is the expectation of a value you're about to receive.
3. The three R's of the Currency of Conversation are:
   Relevance of the message
   Regard for the source
   Resonance with the story at a fundamentally important level
4. The three introspective questions of the Pillars of Purpose upon which the brand architecture is built are:
   Who am I?
   What is my purpose?
   How will I be remembered?
5. The three P's of the Science of Human Connection are:
   Purpose. Stand for something great.
   Passion. Ignite a passion that's contagious.
   Probe. Spot emerging trends, attitudes and behaviour that influence consumer choices.
6. Feelings count for more than facts.
7. Tell emotionally compelling stories based upon shared intangible values.
8. A brand must embody an intangible value deemed hugely important by its users.
9. You can even sell a used toothbrush if it can be the embodiment of something meaningful to others.
10. You can communicate the idea of colour to a blind person only if you perceive it from his "perspective."

INTANGIENCE

INTANGIENCE
INTANGIENCE
INTANGIENCE
INTANGIENCE
INTANGIENCE
INTANGIENCE
INTANGIENCE
INTANGIENCE
INTANGIENCE
INTANGIENCE
INTANGIENCE

INDEX

A

ADDY Awards, 8, 51, 89
advertising
  approaches in, 130–131
  brand of water, 69
  propagandist vs. poignant thinking, 19–21
  reframing challenges, 96
art, value of, 116–118
Art Basel Miami Beach, art fair, 116
assets, tangible vs. intangible, 4
audience attention, media coverage, 80–81

B

Band of Support, initiative, 130
bank
  public relations campaign, 111–114
  "Time is Money" campaign theme, 113
Banks Beer, 56
  Guyana's sense of self, 62
  patriotism, 61

Polar Beer vs., 59
Banks Brewery
challenge, 58
colors of patriotism, 60–62
Guyana, 55–56, 66
Banned by the Media campaign, 73–74
Beetham
basketball court, 88–89
competition by Shaq, 88–89, 92
criminal activity and gang warfare, 83, 85
Benton, Jim, illustration, 20
bottled water, brand, 66–69
bottle of air, Sesame Street character selling, 30–31
brand
bottled water, 66–69
color of connection, 122–124
identity crisis, 56
intangible value, 20–21
Louis Vuitton, 15, 16
market value of ten top, 5
personification of the brand, 57, 58
purpose of, 57–58
brand development, geography of the mind, 55
Burnham, Linden Forbes Sampson, 12–13, 38

C

Cage, John, musical piece titled *4'33*, 117–118, 119
cannibalism, message of, 20
Caribbean, beer campaign, 65–66
Caribbean Community (CARICOM), 63

Caribbean identity
brand, 64–66
forging, 62–64
Carib Brew Caribbean Identity, 64
CARIB Brewery, 62, 64, 104
Carnival
COVID-19 pandemic and celebrations, 96
"Hold On to the Carnival" theme, 97, 109
pandemic of performance, 98–99
Pillars of Purpose, 97–98
Carter, Jimmy, Guyana's standing, 38–39
Carter Center, 38, 39
Catellan, Maurizio, Comedian, 116, 117, 118, 119
Centre for Executive Education, UN's University for Peace, xiii, 9, 99, 131
challenges
reframing, 95–96
shifting perspectives, 124–126
Circle of Consumer Sentiment, 17–18
Clinton, Hillary
campaign slogan, 44
Trump and, 43, 53
Coca-Cola, embodiment of happiness and human connection, 122
Coke, 2–3
brand identity, 65
human connection industry, 68n23
Comedian (Cattelan), 116, 117, 118
Committee for the Reelection of the President (CREEP), 38
connection
color of, 122–124

language of, 2–3, 5–10
consumers, water, 32–33
contraband, roadblock in Guyana, 11–13
Co-Operative Republic of Guyana, 38. See also Guyana
COVID-19 pandemic, Carnival, 96
Currency of Conversation, xv, 6, 7, 141–142
Hoop of Life, 91
intangience insights, 52
relevance, regard, resonance, 26, 43–47, 143

D

De Beers, campaign around diamonds, 106–108
Democratic Party, 78
derivative meaning, concept of, 28–30
diamond industry
ad agency, 106
customer behavior, 106–109
ethical sourcing, 107
lab diamond, 108–109
lab-grown, 107–108
Different (Youngme Moon), 32, 67
disturbances, history of riots as, 41
Dove, advertising, 21

E

Economist, The (magazine), 108
Einstein, Albert, 121
Einstein's theory, 95
election campaign. See also US presidential campaign (2024)
Guyana, 37

Emerson, Ralph Waldo, 111
Emperor's New Clothes, The (Andersen), 117
environmentalists
  hunger strike and, 71, 72–73
  right to protest, 75

F

facts, feelings and, 114–115
feelings, focus on, 114–115
FIJI water, 67
flags, patriotism, 60

G

gang leaders, appeal to "do the right thing," 84
gang violence, campaign addressing, 83–86
geography of the mind, 55
Gift, The, 131
Grenada, National Commercial Bank of, 112–114
Guardian Group, xiii, 98
gun amnesty program, 84
Guyana
  Banks Brewery, 55–56
  Burnham of, 12–13
  candidate's public profile in, 40–41
  colors of patriotism, 60–62
  election campaign, 37
  first female president, 37, 38
  idea of last one to leave blowing out the candle, 41–43
  Jagan as candidate for president, 39–41
  scarcity value, 13–16

sense of self, 62
understanding among ethnic groups, 95–96

H

Haitian immigrants, 77, 78
Happytalism, 100–101, 109
Harris, Kamala, 78, 79
Hoop of Life
competition by Shaq, 88–89, 92
Intangience, 91–93
launch of initiative, 89
Science of Human Connection, 92
TV script, 89–90
how to sell a used toothbrush, 25–28. See also used toothbrush
Hoyte, Desmond, 38, 40, 42, 46
human connection
defining language of, 22
universal language, 137–139
human relationships, industry of, 68n23, 126, 128
hunger strike
environmentalists and, 71, 72
media amplifying the message, 75–78

I

imagination, new color, 123
industry of human relationships, 68n23, 126, 128
intangible assets, tangible vs., 4
intangible value
brand, 20–21
derivative meaning, 33–34

ten top brands, 5
intangience
InvisAbility, 105
lab diamond industry, 108–109
language of human connection, 44
methodology, 7–10
schools of thought, 7
value of, 99
Intangience inquiries
election messages, 53
emotionality of brand, 70
gang leaders' perspective, 93
Hoop of Life, 93
Intangience insights
brand and media coverage, 80–81
brand identity, 64–69
Currency of Conversation, 52
derivative meaning, 33–34
diamonds and consumer behavior, 106–109
everyone needs someone to look up to in life, 87
Hoop of Life initiative, 91–93
meaning and value, 23
meaning of things, 118–119
purpose in life, 135–137
redefining your business, 127–128
InvisAbility, 101–105, 109

J

Jagan, Cheddi, 39
candidate for president, 39–41

expectation of free and fair election, 45
idea of unity and optimism, 41
Jagan, Janet Rosenberg, 38
campaign to carry on husband's legacy, 47–52
first female US-born president of nation, 37, 38
Jagdeo, Bharrat, election campaign of, 47–48
James, LeBron, 79

K

Kamlamania, Trinidad and Tobago, 50
Khaled, DJ, 64
Knot, The, 2025 Real Weddings Study by, 107–108

L

language of connection, 2–3, 5–10
intangience methodology, 7–10
life
meaning in, 129
search for meaning, 119
life of purpose, unconditional love, 139

M

McDonald's, Trump and, 78
Manning, Patrick, Persad-Bissessar and, 50
marketing, brand of water, 67
Martins, Dave, 61
Ministry of National Security
communication campaign, 83, 86, 91
risk of losing hope, 86–91
money

concept of, 115
defining, 114–115
intangible value of, 114
value of, 115
Moon, Youngme, *Different*, 32, 67
movements, creating, 48

N

National Commercial Bank of Grenada, 112–114
National Pizza Day, 127
Nike, 3, 122
Nissan, ad campaign for parts division of, 27–28
Not a Blade of Grass (Martins), 61
N. W. Ayer & Son, De Beers hiring, 106

O

O'Neal, Shaquille, 88, 92

P

Panday, Basdeo, 48
Pandemic of Performance, 109
Carnival, 98–99
Happytalism, 100–101
passion, life, 77, 137, 143
patriotism, colors of, 60–62
People's National Congress, 12
People's National Movement (PNM), 50
"People's Partnership, The," coalition of, 50
People's Progressive Party (PPP), 39, 40, 42, 46
Performance, pandemic of, 98–99

Persad-Bissessar, Kamla, 91
campaign for, 48–49, 51
rise to power, 50
personal illumination, principles, 132–135
personification, brand, 57, 58
persuasion, principles of, 77
Pillars of Purpose, xv, 7, 57, 143
Banks vs. Polar Beer challenge, 59
brand identity, 132–133
Carib Brew, 64
Carnival, 97–98
gang leaders' perspective, 86–87, 91
Pizza Hut, 127
poignant thinking, propagandist thinking vs., 19–22
Polar Beer
Banks vs., 59
illegal import of, 55–56
Venezuela's, 61–62
polyphonic understanding, 77, 100, 137

R

Real Weddings Study (2025), The Knot, 107–108
ReThink, establishment, 130
roses, intangible value on Valentine's Day, 125–126

S

Sabga, Anthony, 102–104, 106
scarcity value, 13–17
Schumpeter, Joseph, concept of money, 115
Science of Human Connection, xiv, xv, 7–8, 10, 17, 52, 142

amplifying the message, 75–78
Hoop of Life, 92
Intangience methodology, 65
Intangience stage as, 136
message resonance, 78–79
polyphonic understanding, 100, 137
principles of persuasion, 77
purpose, passion and probe, 77, 137, 143
shared intangible values and, 69
selling. See used toothbrushes
Sesame Street (television show), Lefty selling Ernie a bottle of air, 30–31
Smuggling, contraband at Guyana roadblock, 11–13
Something only has value when it holds meaning, 16, 23, 93, 118, 141, 143
Super Bowl, advertising, 21

T

tangible assets versus intangible assets, 4
tangible value, ten top brands, 5
toothbrushes. See used toothbrushes
Trump, Donald, 76, 77, 78, 79
Clinton and, 43, 53
presidential election (2024), 77, 78, 79
survival of, 76–77

U

Uber, 128
University for Peace, xiii, 9, 99, 131
unity and optimism, campaign on idea of, 41

universal language, beautiful dream, 137–139
University for Peace, United Nations, xiii, 9, 99, 131
UPEACE Centre, xiii, xiv
used toothbrushes
  art to selling, 25–28
  campaign, 25–26
  exercise for different meaning, 29–30
  how to sell, 25–28
  Nissan parts division, 27–28
  symbol of campaign, 30
US presidential election (2024)
  LeBron James's endorsement of Harris, 79
  message resonance, 78–79
  Trump campaign, 78–79

V

Valentine's Day, intangible value of a rose, 125–126
value
  intangible, 20–21
  life, 23
  market, of top ten brand, 5
  scarcity and, 13–17
Venezuela, border with Guyana, 55, 61
"voiceofthepeople," 49

W

water. See also bottled water
  branding, 31, 32–33
  consumers, 32–33

women's empowerment, 37
worth, value, 17